'Evangelicals in Europe have much to le[...]
developed in other contexts often don't [...]
continent. In *Reconnect Your Church*, David Brown shares insights
gathered over a lifetime of ministry in France and from the exciting revitalisation of a historic church in Paris. I noticed many points of contact
with the ministry challenges I face in Rome. May European churches find
new life by reading this balanced, hopeful and wise book!'
René Breuel, founding pastor of Hopera Church in Rome, Italy, author
of *The Paradox of Happiness*

'David Brown is a well-respected author in the French evangelical world
with a dozen books to his name on subjects ranging from the Trinity to
gender theory. But *Reconnect Your Church* is his first book in English, so
non-francophone readers can finally benefit from his insights and practical advice accumulated over 40 years in ministry, including both church
planting and church revitalisation. David's extensive experience working
with church leaders across Europe means that he is very aware of different
cultural contexts for revitalisation: the process will look very different in
a British city and in a Romanian village! Whatever your context, you will
find gospel-focused wisdom and down-to-earth advice about the process
of church revitalisation in this eminently practical handbook. As part of
a church leadership team in the UK, David's description of a holistically
healthy church frequently caused me to reflect on how and why we do
things. Anyone who cares about the state of their church, both in terms
of its community impact and its role in forming Jesus-centred disciples,
will find much food for thought, prayer and action in this encouraging
book – change is possible and decline is not inevitable!'
Paul Cooke, UK Director of France Mission

'Any book which gives the impression of proposing seven steps to Christian maturity or three keys to a successful marriage raises alarm bells in
my thinking, but this book by my long-time friend, David Brown, is different! Why? Because I have observed David at work for almost half a
century! He has both founded new churches and helped bring to life
dormant existing churches. He knows what are the vital components of a
healthy church and he has clearly and yet compassionately analysed the
obstacles to change in second-generation churches. But, by far his greatest
contribution in my opinion is his grasp of the formidable changes that

have taken place in society and which need to be integrated into any strategy for revitalising the church. On a continent where Christianity is no longer perceived as being relevant, David is on the offensive and with both optimism and realism calls the church to fulfil her role as salt and light.'

Mike Evans PhD, former director of the Geneva Bible Institute, founder of Evangile 21 (European French-speaking branch of The Gospel Coalition)

'In *Reconnect Your Church,* David Brown captures in a very realistic, relevant and biblical way the revitalisation of the church, making readers first aware of the need, but also providing a vision and a process for re-vitalisation. For me, this information, before it was written in a book, took the form of training lectures that David gave in different countries in Europe, including Romania, teaching many church leaders about this topic. I have personally learned a lot about what revitalization is and how it can become a reality in stagnated or declining churches. I guarantee that those who read the book and are ready to act based on it will be helped in a very practical way to experience positive changes in their church.'

Daniel Fodorean, pastor, Associate Professor and Academic Dean at the Baptist Theological Institute of Bucharest

'What a gift to the church! *Reconnect Your Church*, is a theologically rich and intensely practical contribution to the desperately needed, worldwide conversation on church revitalisation. The Euro-centric focus will be espe-cially helpful to a European audience, but will not be a hindrance to other readers. David Brown weaves together a solid biblical foundation, sig-nificant cross-cultural insights, and practical suggestions, all based on his extensive background as a pastor and church planter in France and his broad involvement across the continent. Not surprisingly, the concepts in this book are helpfully applied through the tool of conversations taking place in different European countries. I plan to read this book again . . . and probably again after that. Thank you, David! A job well done!'

Revd Dr Jay Mosser, pastor of Sunset Bible Church, University Place, WA, USA and leader of the European Leadership Forum Disciple-Making Leaders Network

'*Reconnect Your Church* is an encouraging roadmap and expert travel guidebook for church leaders who want to see God do a new thing. If you are asking the Lord to use you in this area, this is the book you need, and David is your conversation partner. David is leading a church revitalization movement across Europe, and this book distils his wisdom. *Read the book and then contact David and join the movement!*'
Greg Pritchard PhD, Director of European Leadership Forum and President of the Forum of Christian Leaders

'David Brown in *Reconnect Your Church* exhibits practical professionalism in the demanding task of church revitalising. The book is inspirational, visionary and educational. It provides a wealth of helpful guidelines to be implemented by any church revitalisation team across Europe. Much needed and timely publication!'
Revd Daniel Trusiewicz, Mission Coordinator, European Baptist Federation

'Across Europe in recent years there has been evidence of significant growth of a new church-planting movement in many countries. There has been much less focus on church revitalisation, some arguing that it is easier to give birth to new body than to attempt to resurrect a dead one! But surely we should do all we can to engage in planting and revitalising? This book fills that gap/ redresses that imbalance. It may be a seminal text; perhaps even a watershed publication for hard-pressed leaders who do not wish to give up on churches which have thrived in the past but which, for whatever reason, have lost their way or drifted in the present.

'Written in the light of widespread experience in France, and in a gracious, unthreatening spirit, David Brown judiciously combines biblical principles, case studies from across Europe, cross-cultural sensitivity, careful research and excellent practical suggestions. It will be studied with great profit by church leadership teams and will likely lead, under God, to the revitalisation of many churches –perhaps even yours!'
Lindsay Brown, former General Secretary, International Fellowship of Evangelical Students (IFES) and International Director of the Lausanne Movement.

'Revitalization is one of the key themes for the renewal of the church in Europe. David Brown is personally involved in the revitalisation process and knows the European context very well. The book is practical, fresh and relevant. I am very grateful, that this book will be useful and inspiring for the renewal process of historic denominations.'
Marián Kaňuch, Lutheran pastor and regional leader, Slovakia

'Every church, no matter it's size, location, culture or context, would benefit from David's insightful understanding and teaching on church revitalisation. His wise counsel is welcome counsel. Revitalisation inevitably means change. David carefully points out barriers to change and offers relevant strategic solutions. His approach is both balanced and biblical, helping churches develop a long-term culture of revitalisation. No church will ever be perfect, but every church can make progress and David lights a fire of hope for my church, your church and every church.'
Scott Poling, Senior Pastor of Harvest New Beginnings Church, USA

'If Europe is to be re-evangelised, it is essential that the opportunities of church planting are accompanied by the opportunities for church revitalisation. David Brown has drawn on a lifetime of experience as a church pastor, planter and revitaliser in urban Paris to write this very helpful guide. He combines a compelling vision for church revitalisation with biblical principles for healthy churches and outlines a practical revitalisation process. A great strength of this book is that he shows, by example, how these general principles can be contextualized in very different circumstances. I pray that this book will be widely read by those with a heart to see the gospel advance in Europe, and that many churches will gain new life and renewed effectiveness as a result.'
John Stevens, National Director FIEC

RECONNECT YOUR CHURCH:

A Practical Handbook
for Church Revitalisation

David Brown

INTER-VARSITY PRESS
36 Causton Street, London SW1P 4ST, England
Email: ivp@ivpbooks.com
Website: www.ivpbooks.com

© David Brown, 2023

Scripture quotations are taken from the New International Version (NIV).

First published 2023

British Library Cataloguing-in-Publication Data
A catalogue record for this book is available from the British Library.

ISBN: 978–1–78974–458–3
eBook ISBN: 978–1–78974–459–0

Set in Minion Pro 10/13.25pt
Typeset in Great Britain by CRB Associates, Potterhanworth, Lincolnshire
Printed in Great Britain by Ashford Colour Press Ltd, Gosport, Hampshire

Produced on paper from sustainable sources

*Inter-Varsity Press publishes Christian books that are true to the Bible and that
communicate the gospel, develop discipleship and strengthen the church for its
mission in the world.*

*IVP originated within the Inter-Varsity Fellowship, now the Universities and Colleges
Christian Fellowship, a student movement connecting Christian Unions in
universities and colleges throughout Great Britain, and a member movement
of the International Fellowship of Evangelical Students. Website: www.uccf.org.uk.
That historic association is maintained, and all senior IVP staff and committee
members subscribe to the UCCF Basis of Faith*

Contents

Acknowledgments

So many people have shaped this book that it would be quite impossible to mention them all.

My thanks go firstly to the members of the Paris-Cardinet church, who were so supportive of my efforts to bring the church back to good health over a period of twelve years and who were willing to try out together many of the ideas which have made their way into this book.

My thinking has also been enriched by so many people whom I have met and interacted with in the Church Revitalisation Network of the European Leadership Forum over the past few years. These participants have come from over twenty-five different countries and that fact in itself has shown me how relevant the teaching of this book is all across Europe but, at the same time, how it has to be applied in different European cultures.

However, I must make special mention of two men who have contributed significantly to my thinking since we met at ELF. Phil Walter of FIEC in the UK was the first man I knew in Europe who was working full-time to revitalise churches. He thoroughly introduced me to the topic and shared a great many practical insights from his experience. And Daniel Fodorean, Academic Dean of the Baptist Theological Institute of Bucharest, has kept me on my toes. It's impossible to chat with Daniel without some new idea or new angle on revitalisation coming up in the conversation.

Many thanks also to Caleb Woodbridge, IVP's publishing director, who has been such a source of wise advice from the time my manuscript was first submitted right through to publication.

And finally, of course, I must express my utmost gratitude to my wife Mary. The word supportive is too weak but that has been the daily reality in my life for over 40 years.

What is the European Leadership Forum (ELF) which has been central in developing the approach to church revitalisation described in this book?

The ELF is a coalition movement that seeks to unite, equip and resource evangelical leaders to renew the biblical church and evangelize Europe.

This happens first at our annual meeting. Here, Forum leaders teach, train and encourage participants from across Europe as everyone seeks to identify common needs and the resources to meet them. Attendees find mentors and build lasting friendships.

Because leaders face unusual challenges due to their vocations and environments, the Forum divides leaders into learning cohorts called Networks, each designed to deal with the unique needs of a specific group of people. Designed to be learning communities of like-minded peers, Networks provide access to specialized training, best practices, and mentoring both at our annual meeting and throughout the year.

Besides the annual meeting, ELF facilitates a variety of other initiatives throughout the year. Forum attendees are also expected to use the resources and partnerships they have gained at the annual meeting to impact their local contexts. Each year, an estimated 800 events, strategies, and partnerships are organized by Forum attendees in their home countries as a result of the annual meeting. These include eight National Forums, which mimic the Forum structure but go one step further by providing contextualized training in national languages.

You can learn more about the ELF by visiting euroleadership.org.

Case studies

All of the names in these scenarios are of course fictitious, and the situations are not drawn from any one church situation.

A small town near Manchester, UK

Sunday breakfast in the Johnson household. The atmosphere was sombre. Tom and Jane were munching their cornflakes slowly and in silence, almost as if they wanted time to stop.

'Why are we always so gloomy on a Sunday morning?' Jane asked suddenly, as if she was making an effort to put into words something that she had been feeling for some time. 'We should be excited at the idea of meeting with the Lord's people for a time of worship together.'

'Worship?' snapped Tom, with sarcasm in his voice as he let his feelings out. He had been bottling them up for too long and now the dam had burst. Maybe they should have had this conversation long ago, but now he was going to get it off his chest. 'We've been going to this church since we got married. At that time, it had a reputation in the town as a lively place. There were loads of other young couples. When they had children, there was a Sunday school for them. And then, later on, the youth group on Saturday evenings was the place to be. Where has it all gone wrong?'

'Well, for one thing,' Jane responded in her usual calm voice (which sometimes annoyed Tom, who recognized that he was far too often prone to impatience), 'most of the young people have gone off to university and then stayed in the city to get a job. You know that's why our own kids are in Manchester and London. And then the closure of the big electrical appliance factory has had a big impact on the town. Sure, the congregation has been decreasing for years, but we must be faithful, Tom. That's what God expects of us.'

'Faithful? If you mean that we have to go through the motions every week, singing the same old songs, hearing the same Bible texts preached on week in week out by the elders. That's not worship for me! Yes, they're elders — because they're even older than us, I suppose.'

'Now you're being disrespectful, Tom. That won't get us anywhere. But I know what you mean. I want to be challenged. I want to be amazed at what our God has done for us. Remember when we were in the Christian Union all those years ago at university? Those Saturday evening meetings left my heart singing for a week as we looked at the Bible together. But I'm not sure that we can do anything about it in our church now.'

'OK. I'm sorry, Jane. But I want to leave if nothing changes. I feel trapped, but it'd be such a disappointment for everyone if we left. We're in our early sixties, but most of the congregation think of us as the young members! I should've shared it at the time, but at our last members' meeting I could've screamed when the only thing talked about was the state of the building and the budget they'd need for renovations. God has called us to fight sin, not woodworm. It's as if the idea of someone becoming a Christian and joining the church is no longer imaginable.'

A city in the west of France

Sunday breakfast in the Marchal household. The atmosphere was sombre. Guillaume and Valérie were munching their croissants slowly and in silence, almost as if they wanted time to stop.

'I'm exhausted,' Guillaume managed to find the energy to say. 'We only had five hours' sleep last night after we got back from Julien's place.' There was a pause. 'It was a great party, wasn't it?' Another pause, longer this time. 'But now they expect us to get up for the Sunday service at ten o'clock! That's an unearthly time for people of our generation. I know that people with kids have already been up for hours and that's fine for them. But what about us? We both have demanding jobs. We hardly have time to see each other during the week. I only leave my screen for a moment and the emails begin to build up. The phone rings all day long. I just want some peace and quiet at the weekend. Some time for myself. For us.'

Valérie nodded her head in agreement. It was a bit early in the day to get into a long conversation, but she smiled ruefully. She understood what her husband was going through. They had only been married for a couple of years but she knew his love for the Lord (that's what had attracted her to him in the first place) and his frustration at the way that their church functioned. The Sunday morning service was quite lively and Guillaume would be the first to admit it. There were guitars, drums and various other instruments and they often sang the latest praise songs. But he didn't feel able to invite his friends to that type of worship. He thought that they would be embarrassed to have to stand and sing words that they didn't truly believe with a smile on their lips and their arms in the air.

'Why, oh why, *ma chérie*, can't we have a different sort of service on a Sunday evening when our friends are awake and have nothing else to do?' Guillaume dipped his croissant into his coffee and answered his own question. 'I know, they think that they're a vibrant, state-of-the-art church. But they don't realize that times have changed, and what's modern for their generation isn't so relevant for us. Thirty years have gone by since the church was planted and it has been successful – I grant you that. But what I don't understand is why the leaders aren't prepared to experiment. I've looked through the church archives and I saw in the photos that they were our age when they started the church. They were thought of as radical, hot-headed idealists at that time. Now we must all be careful not to change anything, not to harm the church's reputation.'

A village in central Romania

Sunday breakfast in the Constantinescu household. The atmosphere was sombre. Stefan and Ana were munching their ham and cheese slowly and in silence, almost as if they wanted time to stop.

'I don't want to go to church this morning,' sighed Stefan.

'But you have to, darling,' Ana replied. 'You're the pastor.' This was their little joke, which they had been repeating every Sunday morning for the past few months. 'I'll go and wake the boys,' said Ana. Their twin sons, Alexandru and Mihai, were sixteen years old. At that age, you couldn't expect them to wake up eagerly on a Sunday morning.

'No. Just wait a moment, Ana. I'm serious. What are we going to do? Should I ask to be transferred to another church in our denomination? I don't think that I can go on like this for much longer.'

Ana looked at him tenderly. She knew how hard he worked and how seriously he took his calling to be a pastor. She respected his commitment to God and his love of the gospel, but she was also a realist.

'My love,' she said, 'I don't think that will help. You're not likely to get a pastorate in a city at this stage of life, and you know that all the rural churches are in the same state as ours.'

'But how can we change things? I'm not trying to turn the world upside down, especially in a village like ours. But I feel sorry for our boys. They're the only ones under thirty in our congregation. It's been six years since we moved here, and I can't remember anyone being converted who wasn't already connected to the church. It's disheartening.'

'But we can't give up now,' Ana tried to encourage her husband. 'Surely we can do something?'

'Yes, but I don't know what. These people need the gospel but they seem so indifferent. Their work, their families, eating and drinking at weekends – that's what makes up their lives. They've given up on religion, as long as we're there occasionally to meet their needs with weddings and funerals.'

'Couldn't we start a prayer meeting to pray for the village?'

'I suggested it at the last church council meeting but the idea got buried in the mass of unimportant things on the agenda,' he dismissed. 'But, you know, this is what truly hurts me. Over in the next village, a group of young people is planting a new church. They publish articles about church growth and pour scorn on the long-established churches, saying that we're not reaching out to non-believers with the gospel. But most of their congregation is drawn from our existing churches! They aren't any more successful than we are in bringing unchurched people to the Lord.'

Introduction

The same pattern that we see in these stories can be recognized all over Europe.[1] Unfortunately, many churches need new life so that we, as Christians, can be encouraged to live from day to day with our wonderful God. But this new life must also be attractive to those around us. All too often, Christianity is viewed as negative, intolerant, judgmental and legalist. In my cynical moments, I catch myself thinking that it is as if people hear us saying, 'I'm not allowed to do this thing as a Christian. Why don't you become a Christian, and you won't be allowed to do it either!' Thank God that there are many exciting things happening across Europe. There are many vibrant churches, particularly in cities with a large student population.

I haven't written this book primarily for these fellowships but for the many struggling churches. If this describes your church, then this book is for you. It has been written to help those churches reconnect, in particular those with plateauing or declining congregations who do not feel able to reach out to their surrounding area with the gospel. The potential that could be released through revitalising these churches is huge.

What is needed? This book does not offer easy answers, instead suggesting that the way forward is a combination of *vision* and *process*.

First of all, a church needs a *vision* that takes the realities of the local situation and today's culture into consideration, but that starts from first principles by taking God's Word seriously. What is more fundamental than the greatest commandments that Jesus taught? In other words, the spiritual aspect of our lives (loving God with all our heart, soul, mind and strength), the social aspect of our lives (loving one another as believers) and the societal aspect of our lives (loving our neighbours in today's context). God's priorities can seem almost too obvious, but I was encouraged by an email I received from a man who had attended a seminar I led

---

1 I have written this book from a European perspective but the approach that I describe may well have relevance to Christians elsewhere around the world, particularly where churches are struggling to connect in post-Christian and increasingly secular contexts.

on revitalisation. He wrote, 'It takes years of experience and a lot of thought to be able to summarize the complex issues so well.' Far from being a list of handy tips or management techniques, church leaders across Europe have found the approach in this book to be more cutting-edge than it may appear at first sight. 'It was obvious . . . and yet we did it,' could be their motto.

Second, the church has to go through a *process* of revitalisation. There is no such thing as a 'quick fix' and there never has been. Nearly everything in life is accomplished step by step, but having an objective helps us to go in the right direction and motivates us to keep moving. This process takes into account the fact that there will be resistance to change and acknowledges that some churches may be more flexible than others, but the aim of the church leaders is to take as many people as possible with them towards the vision of a healthy church, leading to a greater love for God and for others to the glory of Jesus Christ.

I must stress that, when I use the word 'process', I do not mean that there is a procedure to follow or a set of steps that will automatically lead to revitalisation. Europeans are slightly allergic to that way of thinking (compared to our American cousins). I could have chosen the word 'implementation' instead of 'process' to avoid misunderstanding but, for the sake of convenience, I have retained 'process' throughout the book. Please remember that I never view revitalisation as a sequence of events with a guaranteed outcome. Revitalisation is more of an art than a science. And in any case, the outcome ultimately rests on the work of the Holy Spirit in our churches and prayer is an important part of the whole process.

Throughout Europe today, hope has become a rare commodity. But I believe that the revitalisation of our churches is possible. Christians are people of hope: 'Let us hold unswervingly to the hope we profess, for he who promised is faithful' (Hebrews 10:23).

1

My revitalisation story

How did I become involved in church revitalisation? Why has it become a major part of my ministry? Let me tell you a bit about myself since we're going on this journey together.

I was born in England and brought up in a churchgoing family but it wasn't until I went to university in Bristol that I became a Christian. During my first week as a student, I was invited to join a Christian Union Bible study group. I was challenged by the book we were studying: Paul's letter to the Galatians. I must have said something blatantly humanistic (I thought at that time that humans were intrinsically good) because one young man pointed out strongly that there is no other gospel than the one preached by the apostle: the grace of Christ who gave himself for our sins (see Galatians 1:3–9). I bought and devoured John Stott's *Basic Christianity*.[1] Then, one Sunday evening, I attended a special meeting at which the preacher walked us through the Ten Commandments. I remember thinking at first, 'What a pity that my non-Christian friends aren't here to hear this!' but, as the evening went on, I was more and more convicted of sin and prayed that, if I wasn't really a Christian, I would become one and have assurance of my salvation. I date my Christian life from that evening.

I was studying French at university because I had been attracted to French culture all through my teenage years. I spent hours at home listening to French radio and reading French books but, coming from a family of modest means, I had never set foot outside England. Three months after my conversion, my course took me to Bordeaux for a semester, so two-thirds of my first nine months as a Christian were spent in France. In fact, as I got off the train when I arrived in Paris on my way to Bordeaux, I looked around and the thought came to me, 'You've come

---

1 John Stott, *Basic Christianity* (London: IVP, 2012).

home.' This conviction has never left me. My wife, our children and I took French citizenship thirty years ago. I sometimes say that I was only born in England through a heavenly administrative error.

By the end of my time at university, I was a qualified language teacher and, after three years teaching at a secondary school in Bristol, I moved to France after finding a job in the city of Nancy in Lorraine (eastern France). That is where I became a 'missionary' through the back door. A Bible study in our home developed into a church and I was accepted as a church planter by a French group of churches called France Mission (now called Perspectives).

For the next three decades, that was my main ministry. I planted two churches in the Nancy region (Vandoeuvre and Villers-lès-Nancy), the area where my four children were born. Then we moved to Paris, where I joined the leadership team of France Mission. During this time, I also planted a church in Le Blanc-Mesnil, a northeastern suburb of Paris. From 2003 until 2016, I led the Groupes Bibliques Universitaires (GBU), the student movement affiliated with the International Fellowship of Evangelical Students (IFES), for nine years as general secretary and then for four years as the chair of the board. In those thirteen exciting years, I came back to my roots (I became a Christian at university) as we developed apologetic tools and evangelistic outreach to French students.

But I could not leave my first love: pastoring a church. Even during those years, I was appointed as the pastor of a church in central Paris. That seems a fairly banal thing to write but, for me, this was an entirely new development because it was not a church plant. My wife, Mary, and I had never known any church ministry that wasn't a 'start-up', as they say in business circles. So why did we go to this church? Quite simply, because the Lord called us to.

When I first heard the news that this church would have to shut down unless someone came to lead it, I could not believe my ears. The church had been founded at the end of the nineteenth century and had been in newly acquired well-situated premises for only ten years. But there had been a church split. Half the members had left, people were discouraged and there was no leadership team, just one elder with a very time-consuming job who did not feel that he could take on the burden of the church alone.

I was ministering to students on the Caribbean island of Martinique when a pastor there told me about the situation. He had attended the Paris church during his time as a student at an evangelical theological faculty.

On our return home, I met with a member of the church whom I knew, a former elder then in his eighties, and we agreed that my name should be put to the church as their next pastor, even if it was only part-time because of my involvement with the student movement.

So this is where my personal story meets church revitalisation. Except that, at that time, no one had ever heard the word 'revitalisation'. I fell back on a word that made sense to me with my past experience. I told the congregation that we would have to 'replant' the church. As time went by, I realized that the need to bring new life to churches was moving up the agenda in the USA. For a few months in 2015 and 2016, I had some unexpected secretarial help, so I asked her to research revitalisation on the internet. She found dozens of websites, blogs and books, none of which had made much of an impact in Europe.

I was struck particularly by some statistics concerning the situation in the USA, mainly based on research done in Southern Baptist churches:[2]

- 10–15% of churches were healthy and multiplying
- 70–75% of churches were plateauing or declining
- 10–15% of churches were at or near risk of disappearing

I was curious to know whether the same figures were seen in France, where there has been a great increase in the number of evangelicals over the past few decades. It is estimated that the number of evangelical believers rose from just 50,000 in 1950 to 650,000 in 2020, and that (on average) a new evangelical church has been planted in France every ten days over the past fifty years. In 1970, there were 840 evangelical churches but that increased to more than 2,500 churches in 2020.[3]

Considering this remarkable growth, I wondered whether church revitalisation was even necessary in France. Rather than attempt a strictly scientific survey, I decided to contact church leaders directly. As the chair of the Evangelism Commission of the Conseil national des évangéliques de France (the CNEF or, in English, the French National Council of Evangelicals), I wrote to the leaders of all the denominations affiliated with our

---

2 You can find more detail and discussion of these figures at "Healthy, Growing Churches," www.caskeycenter.com/2016/09/23/healthy-growing-churches (accessed 13/06/22).

3 These figures are based on research conducted by the missiologist Daniel Liechti for the CNEF. You can read more about this work (in French) at "CNEF 1 pour 10000," www.1pour10000.fr.

movement and asked them to give me their (admittedly subjective) opinion on how they would place the congregations in their fellowship in the categories used by the American survey. The results clearly showed the need for revitalisation.

This is a summary of the answers I received from the denominations:

- 51% of churches were healthy and multiplying
- 38% of churches were plateauing or declining
- 11% of churches were at or near risk of disappearing

I was relieved to find that the statistics were more encouraging than those from the other side of the Atlantic, but I was struck by the fact that half of our churches were not progressing in numbers and that over 10% were at risk of simply disappearing.

This led me to think of our priorities in France. Since its inception, the CNEF has promoted church-planting vigorously, using the slogan 'one for ten thousand'. Even the French secular media has taken on board that our objective is to establish enough new churches that there would be one evangelical church for an average of 10,000 people nationwide. This is a very ambitious aim in a nation that was traditionally Roman Catholic and is now extremely secular. However, as I pondered these statistics, it struck me that we would never reach this target if existing churches disappeared at the rate that new churches were planted.

Fortunately, revitalisation is now on the radar. The CNEF organized a useful interdenominational learning community over a period of two years and several groups of churches are now committed to seeing new life in their congregations.

However, my personal story does not end there. Since 2014, I have been attending the annual meetings of the European Leadership Forum, a network for evangelical leaders across Europe, which meets in Poland. During this time, it has become gradually clear to the forum leaders that church revitalisation should be put on the agenda, so I started running webinars in the year-round mentoring programme. At the 2018 forum, we held our full-scale Revitalisation Network for the first time.

This European initiative has continued to enrich my thinking on revitalisation, as I have talked with participants, been invited to lead seminars on the subject, coached churches and taught at pastoral training and theological institutes in various countries such as (at the time of writing) Switzerland, Lithuania, Poland, Albania, Serbia, Slovakia and Romania.

If there is one thing I would like to stress at the outset of this book, it is that there are no easy answers and no one-size-fits-all solutions. This is partly because we have to bear four variables in mind.

The region within Europe

What I am about to write contains some big generalizations, but I have identified three areas of Europe, each with a different history that affects their approach to revitalisation:

- Northwest Europe (for example, Scandinavia, the Netherlands, the UK and Germany), where there are often old churches and old church buildings that were built for another time.
- Central and Eastern Europe, where churches may well comprise three generations of believers coming from three different eras: the older members who lived through the persecution of soviet times; the baby boomers who were part of a big wave of conversions after the fall of communism; and the younger generations who share the mindset of the postmodern, materialistic young people in Western Europe.
- Southern Europe where, against a Catholic background, evangelicalism is fairly new as a visible option. The majority of churches have been planted over the past fifty years and the leaders have not always passed the baton to the next generation.

The ecclesiastical tradition

The approach to revitalisation may be quite different in the so-called Free Churches (Baptist, Brethren, Pentecostal etc.) as compared to the historic denominations originating at the time of the Reformation (Presbyterian, Lutheran). This is particularly the case where leadership and decision-making processes are concerned.

City, town or rural area

The context of the church implies that what is possible or desirable in a big city will not be applicable in a village and vice versa. Although the principles of revitalisation remain the same as I develop them in this book, the way in which they are implemented in different local situations will need careful thought and contextualization.

The stage that the church is at

There are three key moments for revitalisation in the life cycle of a church. These are illustrated by the following diagram:

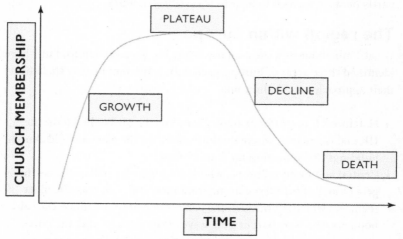

Figure 1 **The church membership curve over time**

- First, the so-called stable church: after a period of growth, things plateau. At this point, according to many experts, changes are needed to prevent an inevitable decline.
- Then, the church in crisis: decline is happening and people are beginning to realize this with some degree of apprehension.
- Finally, the church in danger of dying: the church has declined to the point where it is in fact no longer viable due to the small numbers attending and/or the age of the leadership. I have a photo on my desk to remind me of this danger. It is a picture of an animal, the Tasmanian tiger, which became extinct on 7 September 1936 when the last living specimen died in Hobart Zoo. This picture reminds me to pray that churches would not just disappear, all the more so because Christian men and women have laboured over the years to establish and maintain these communities of believers.

This book has come out of my personal experience in a specific urban context in Paris and from a great number of conversations and a great deal of input from France and from across Europe. It comes out of the conviction that church revitalisation and church-planting are both vitally necessary ministries.

I dislike the idea that I have heard some church planters affirm: 'It is easier to give birth than to raise the dead.' First, because it is not true – I can vouch for that. Second, because it is not realistic. We know that there is a cyclical movement in every aspect of human life and that renewal is possible. Recently, I was present at a speech made by my local member of Parliament in which he stated that he was working towards the revitalisation of an area of our city. Yes, he used that very word! Third, because no church planter foresees the day when the church that he or she is working hard to plant will begin to lose its impetus and need revitalisation.

However, before we move further, I should make it clear that numbers are not the most important thing. I realize that this chapter has mainly shown the need for revitalisation by quoting figures and talking about decreasing numbers, but the aim of revitalisation is to bring new life. In fact, the Latin root of this word, *vita*, means life. 'Will you not give us new life that your people may rejoice in you?' (Psalm 85:6, my translation).

So if it is not primarily about size, what is the main issue? The title of the book shows what is at stake. We need to reconnect.

First, we need to reconnect to God because our Western society seems to be designed to make him unnecessary. Our culture is used to self-sufficiency and material plenty. No one expects to come to work on Monday morning and hear the boss say, 'Hey, we've got a difficult week ahead of us. Maybe we should start with a time of prayer?' at least unless they work for a church or Christian organization. And why pray for our daily bread when we can just go to the local supermarket and buy some? Our comfortable Western assumptions have perhaps been challenged by Covid-19, war, and their economic impacts but we still tend towards self-reliance. We have to relearn how to live in the presence of God and how to trust in him alone in our post-Christian context.

Second, the Covid-19 pandemic that began in 2020 helped to remind us of the importance of relationships through the way in which they were disrupted by lockdowns, leaving us with the challenges of reconnecting afterwards. Of course not everything was negative. In some cases, new relationships were forged across frontiers and extended families spent more time together online than they used to spend meeting face to face. Online meetings made church more accessible to certain groups of people such as those with disabilities and those who live far from vibrant churches. Our challenge now is to think about how we can continue to include these people. But fundamentally, there is something in us that longs for deeper connection with other people. Churches are good places to find that.

There is also a third need for reconnection. Some observers talk about a disconnect between churches and society, a distance between what Christians believe and the way that other people see the world. Christians need to reconnect, share God's love in a meaningful way and communicate the good news in a way that looks like good news.

The end result of reconnection will be a healthy church. For the purposes of this book, and to see where we will be going in the process of revitalisation, here is my definition of a healthy church. It is extremely simple and therefore memorable and inspiring because it is, I believe, a summary of what Jesus and the apostles taught about the church as the people of God living in this abnormal, God-rejecting world:

> A healthy church is a fellowship of believers, redeemed through the gospel, who are learning to love God with all their heart, with all their soul, with all their mind, with all their strength (see Mark 12.30) and to love people (see Mark 12:31) in their cultural context.

This is what Jesus taught when he identified the most important commandments. It has been the continual challenge for Christians who have faced each new cultural context as the church spread from Jerusalem into the pagan Roman Empire, and then to the ends of the earth, and then as cultures developed through the centuries. That is why I believe that revitalisation must include these three simultaneous dimensions of a healthy church:

1 the spiritual aspect of loving God
2 the social aspect of loving others
3 the societal aspect in our context

This threefold concept of revitalisation is wider than the traditional understanding of revival, in particular the concept of revival that is often part of our evangelical heritage. Revivals tend to focus on the spiritual experience of believers and emphasize the individual's need to move to a higher spiritual plane. I believe that the New Testament teaching on Christian life centres on the church as a body and on the ordinary day-to-day life of the disciple. The title of the classic book written by Eugene Peterson says it all: *A Long Obedience in the Same Direction*.[4] The subtitle is also revealing: *Discipleship in an Instant Society*.

As I go on, I will unpack these three aspects as we look at revitalisation as a process that concerns the whole church, which results in a healthy church.

---

4 Eugene Peterson, *A Long Obedience in the Same Direction: Discipleship in an Instant Society* (London: IVP, 2021).

2
The need for revitalisation

The end result of revitalisation is a healthy church. As far as we humans are concerned, health is an important issue in today's world. Not just treating illness and, if possible, curing diseases, but the concept of 'wellness'. An incredible number of books, websites and podcasts offer advice on keeping fit and well. They cover everything from physical exercise and eating patterns to mindfulness and relationships. One of the most important factors is regular check-ups to screen for potential illnesses before they develop. If someone is in denial and does not seek treatment, the situation will not improve and it can sadly lead to premature death. This happened to the mother of a friend of mine. She did not tell her family about the cancerous growths in her body and when she finally saw a doctor it was too late. The same is true for a church. No one will take action to revitalise a church unless they realize that there is a problem.

While I was still pondering how to go about revitalising my church in Paris, I discovered a book by an American author, Thom S. Rainer. The title speaks for itself: *Autopsy of a Deceased Church: 12 Ways to Keep Yours Alive*.[1] I warmly recommend this book to you.

Here are some of the 'symptoms' that Rainer detects, which can form the basis of a church check-up. His words are in italics and I have added some personal thoughts to each indicator:

- *'Slow erosion'*
  The gradual erosion of numbers can happen so slowly that the church members do not realize it is happening. But a visitor who knew the church several years ago can see it when he or she comes back.

---

1 Thom S. Rainer, *Autopsy of a Deceased Church: 12 Ways to Keep Yours Alive* (Nashville, TN: B & H, 2014).

- *'The past is the hero'*
  I remember being in a Baltic country where a pastor told me how
  open people were to spiritual things after the fall of communism.
  At that time, he and the church members would go out on the streets
  on a Sunday afternoon with a couple of guitars and invite people to
  come to their meeting place to hear the gospel. People did, but the
  context is very different now. Postmodern thought is omnipresent
  in the media and materialism gives people a lot of options for how
  they use their time. Today it is very unlikely that a young person
  in that country would follow a guitar player through the streets to
  a church meeting. But – and here's the problem – this pastor told
  me that several older people in the church think that the drop in
  the number of conversions is due to a reluctance to use this method
  of evangelism.
- *'The Church refuses to look like the community'*
  This seems to come mainly from the feeling that society is going
  from bad to worse and that the church should be a citadel, a fortress,
  into which Christians can retreat for protection from the evil world.
  This idea is not new. Recently, I picked up a book published more
  than fifty years ago in which the opening sentence talked about
  'the ruinous times we live in'. There are indeed good biblical grounds
  for us to be on our guard (for example, 2 Peter 3:3 warns against
  the scoffers who will come in the last days). But the 'good old days'
  (whenever exactly you look to) were often mixed with great sin
  on the part of both Christians and the wider world, such as the open
  support of slavery and racism. There has never been a pure golden
  age, but the call remains to be witnesses and to adapt as far as
  possible to the people around us in order to avoid creating a barrier
  that prevents them from understanding the gospel. As Christ's
  ambassadors (see 2 Corinthians 5:20) Christians must speak with the
  authority of the King, but with enough graciousness and connection
  (an ambassador is a diplomat, after all) so that people hear the
  message, which it is our responsibility to communicate.
- *'The budget moved inwardly'*
  This means that the church budget becomes focused on maintenance
  and the comfort of the church members rather than on the needs
  of those outside the church. In particular, there is often too much
  emphasis on preserving the way that the church building looks. Jesus

said, 'For where your treasure is, there your heart will be also'
(Matthew 6:21).

- 'The Preference-Driven Church'
  In other words, church the way I like it! Rainer is alluding to
  the well-known book *The Purpose-Driven Church*,[2] but with an
  enormous change. Instead of building the church around objectives,
  the church has become a place where the members put their needs
  first (for example, my music style, my time and length of worship
  service and my preferred type of Bible study). As a young Christian,
  I was taught that joy in Christianity came from the right order of
  priorities: J, for Jesus first; O, for others next; Y, for yourself last.
  But, in a dying church, this has been forgotten. I remember a pastor
  in an Eastern European country telling me that their worship
  service often included a brass band and that he could not persuade
  the church members to change this, though most non-Christians
  would probably prefer another style of music as a way to approach
  God. It reminds me of the old joke: What's the difference between
  a terrorist and the worship leader in a church? You can negotiate
  with a terrorist.
- 'The Great Commission becomes the Great Omission'
  Jesus told us after his resurrection that we should go and make
  disciples of all nations, baptizing them and teaching them
  (see Matthew 28:19). Bringing the gospel to the ends of the earth
  and to our neighbours is a sign of a healthy church. The way that
  we do it is not important, but a heart to do it is. A healthy church
  supports and prays for the spread of the gospel in other countries
  and encourages all church members to do the same in their local
  environments.

In fact, I think that the problem can sometimes be even more serious:
amnesia regarding the gospel itself, even in so-called gospel churches.
I have attended services where Jesus and the gospel were barely mentioned
in the songs, the prayers or the sermon. How has this come about? It is
probably when the leaders and members of a church reach the point where
the gospel is the tacit foundation, merely assumed and not clearly articu-
lated. No one denies the gospel and it is still part of the church's declaration

---

2 Rick Warren, *The Purpose Driven Church* (Grand Rapids, MI: Zondervan, 1995).

of faith, but it is no longer what people are excited about, it is no longer central. Other things have become more important, for example, the building, a certain style of worship, hanging on to the young people, or the social programmes. This is perilous because the next generation may well lose sight of the gospel itself.

I want to say a word about the gospel since this book takes the gospel to be central. The apostle Paul summarized the gospel in his first letter to the church in Corinth: 'For what I received I passed on to you as of first importance: that Christ died for our sins according to the Scriptures, that he was buried, that he was raised on the third day according to the Scriptures' (1 Corinthians 15:3–4). Why are these facts of first importance? Because 'by this gospel you are saved' (1 Corinthians 15:2). To be saved (or 'our salvation') means to escape from danger, such as to be saved from drowning. But from the biblical perspective, the danger is to remain an enemy of God because of our sin, to have no relationship with the one who is the source of life and to be judged by him at the end of our earthly life. The result is that such people 'will be punished with everlasting destruction and shut out from the presence of the Lord' (2 Thessalonians 1:9). The good news (which is the meaning of the word 'gospel') is that we can be saved from this disaster by putting our trust in Jesus. When he died in our place, he suffered the judgment that we deserve so that we could be forgiven, though God took our sin so seriously that he had to punish it. 'It is by grace you have been saved, through faith' (Ephesians 2:8). The grace of God is everything we do not deserve but he gives it to us because of his burning love for us.

Salvation is not only being saved from danger but also the blessings of being made righteous in Christ. We can enjoy knowing God all through our lives on this earth and forever as his adopted children (see Ephesians 1). When he returns to restore all creation under his kingly rule (see Romans 8), we will live with him forever in the new creation (Revelation 21).

That is why we have the privilege to bear Jesus' name as Christians and that is why everything that we do should be focused on him so that he receives honour, glory and praise.

Much of this book describes the down-to-earth process of revitalisation, involving the complicated lives of people who are saved but not yet perfect. But we should always bear in mind that our aim is to be constantly Christ-centred. Thom Rainer's book continues:

- *'The church rarely prayed together'*
  Times of open prayer had been replaced by 'a word of prayer'. In any case, this is the logical next step from the amnesia regarding the Great Commission. Church prayer must not be focused solely on the aches and pains of believers while the needs of the world are forgotten.
- *'The church had no clear purpose'*
  For me, this is very sad. It is as if the members are playing a game called church and just going through the motions. Everything is predictable. Nothing is ever surprising. There is no sense of wonder, no excitement that the Holy Spirit may lead in unexpected ways, no amazement at the greatness of God or at the breathtaking salvation through grace, which we have in Jesus. The reason for this is quite simple. The church has forgotten its biblical, gospel-centred purpose – its *raison d'être*, as we say in French: the reason for its very existence.

In addition to these symptoms identified by Rainer, I would add another, which I have often observed in Europe: legalism. This is an approach to the Christian life focused on trying to please God by an outward conformity to his law, though often in ways that go beyond what the Bible requires by being based on human traditions (see Colossians 2:20–23) rather than on the inner spiritual reality of loving God and depending on his forgiveness and grace. I remember saying in an Eastern European country that a very good stimulus to revitalisation is the presence of a newly born-again Christian in the church. I gave the example of a young woman from my own church who was telling all her non-Christian friends about her conversion. Even her boss was asking her on Monday mornings, 'What did your pastor talk about yesterday?' I mentioned that she was also struggling to stop smoking but said that I felt that was less important than her love for the people around her. At that point, one of the men listening to me objected that a true Christian would not smoke and quoted 1 John: 'No one who is born of God will continue to sin' (1 John 3:9).

This attitude is not limited to Eastern Europe. In any organization that is facing decline, the temptation to 'batten down the hatches' increases. This is a nautical term. The hatches (or hatchways) were the openings on the deck that allowed air inside the ship. In bad weather, these were covered with tarpaulins to stop water from coming in and the tarpaulins were attached to the deck with strips of wood known as battens. The aim is to reduce the possible cause of problems. What better way to do this than by demanding a strict adherence to rules, even if the rules are man-made? Jesus spoke strongly against this: 'You nullify the word of God by your tradition that you have handed down' (Mark 7:13).

All of these different symptoms fit into a pattern that can be observed in the life of churches. Sometimes the process can happen over just a few years. Sometimes it takes decades. But in order to revitalise a church, it is important to understand this process. We already alluded to this in the diagram of the church membership curve in chapter 1.

What does the typical life cycle of a church look like?

The beginning

The church is born out of a vision and a need. A visionary, a mission or a group of like-minded people recognize the need for a Bible-based church (or sometimes a church with a particular theological persuasion) in a certain area and make the decision to plant one. This might have happened as recently as the past twenty to thirty years but the church may be much older than that.

The growth phase

The initial vision is clear: the aim is to build up a church and to bring it to maturity with a viable number of participants. In our French situation, this would be between forty and sixty adults with a recognized govern-ance (meaning a pastoral team and a religious association declared to the civil authorities). This implies financial independence and a permanent place to meet, often involving the purchase of premises at some sacrificial cost in time and money from the members.

At the outset, the membership is often composed of young couples or young families with small children and a few single people, with one or two mature Christians who give leadership to the group. Church life is characterized by a certain freedom from organizational traditions. Everyone knows everyone and there is a high level of commitment. New people join the church naturally if they are in the same age bracket and have the same social background. At the same time, the church makes a real effort to reach people outside the church fellowship. Evangelism is high on the agenda. All in all, there is a good balance between three dif-ferent aspects of discipleship: serving God, serving the church and serving the world.

The mature church phase

When the critical size of the group (between forty and sixty adults) is reached, the feeling that the job is done can creep in. The idea of growth becomes less important because the needs of the Christians come to the forefront and take centre stage. The structuring of the church becomes the priority and provision is needed for the children and teenagers of the founding members. A church council is elected to help run the church and other activities are given a more organized structure, for example, the worship group starts a formal rota, including people to run the sound system and project the words onto the screen.

This structural organization of the church puts demands on the time and availability of the most committed people in the fellowship. The need to see conversions is felt less keenly due to the size of the existing group, which is self-sufficient. A church with a building also attracts believers from other churches and Christians moving into the area because of the quality of its activities. These focus on teaching and worship rather than on evangelism. The church is a place where you feel good.

The phase of decline

At this point, we begin to see the lack of missiological reflection on the church and its environment. The same methods of evangelism that worked at the start of the church are still used but only a handful of discouraged volunteers run these activities.

The building itself is aging: the chairs, the paintwork and decoration, the reception area and the sound system. The same song collection is used. Almost nothing has changed since the day that the building was inaugurated. The only innovations are due to the aging congregation, for example, setting up daytime activities for retired members. In rural areas, the young people leave the church in order to study or work in cities.

In a word, there is no longer any vision. The church no longer lives, it just functions. Worse still, without vision, tensions between people may crystallize around insignificant details, especially when change is involved. It can even happen that the original leaders may prefer to see the church die with them rather than accept another way of doing things.

To return to our health check-up, what signs should we be looking for in order to see the need for revitalisation? Here is a non-exhaustive list:

- Christians no longer dare to invite people from outside the church because the culture of the church has become completely inaccessible to the uninitiated.
- The numbers of people attending the church decrease.
- The average age of the church members increases.
- Structures and activities are talked about more often than life in Christ.
- Family dynasties govern the church and make it virtually impossible for newcomers to take part in leadership.
- A culture of unspoken taboos has taken hold so it becomes impossible to question anything in the life of the church.
- There is resistance to change, even minor changes.
- A culture of triumphalism has taken root: everything is fine, all the problems come from 'the world' and people do not seem to appreciate what the church is doing.

As we come to the end of this chapter on the need for revitalisation, it is clear that there are countless ways in which a church can be unhealthy, countless ways of being sick. Let's remind ourselves of what a healthy church is. Here is the definition I gave in chapter 1:

A healthy church is a fellowship of believers, redeemed through the gospel, who are learning to love God with all their heart, with all their soul, with all their mind, with all their strength (Mark 12:30) and to love people (Mark 12:31) in their cultural context.

Why is church revitalisation so important? I think that there are three reasons:

1 So that God can be glorified and recognized for who he truly is and that his name (which represents all he is) can be honoured and respected as Jesus encouraged us to request in the Lord's Prayer, which he taught his disciples (see Matthew 6:9).
2 So that Christians can flourish in every aspect of their lives. 'Grow in the grace and knowledge of our Lord and Saviour Jesus Christ' (2 Peter 3:18).
3 So that non-Christians can see that our faith is plausible. What does it mean for something to be plausible? It is when something is not

immediately dismissed as being impossible and when people think it worth considering. Our Christian apologetics have traditionally dealt with the credibility, rather than the plausibility, of our faith by asking the questions, 'Is it true? Can it be believed?' There is of course a real place for this, but it cannot be the starting point today.

I saw this very clearly in a non-Christian context in France when the government was dealing with a wave of protests by a group that became known as the *gilets jaunes* (meaning yellow jackets). Here are some quotations from politicians belonging to the ruling party:

- 'We are not on the same wavelength. They have feelings, we have arguments, we are not connecting.'
- 'It is very difficult to have a constructive dialogue. People are not rational.'
- 'I have factual arguments, but my arguments are not strong enough to deal with their feeling of desperation.'

These statements could well have been made by Christians trying to witness to their friends.

We have to understand the way in which people process information today. In summary, we can state it in the following way:

Plausibility leads to *desirability* leads to *credibility*

In other words:

I must check this out — I like it — Is it true?

These three reasons for making our churches healthy are like a 'loop' in computer programming. If our Christian lives – individually and collectively – are flourishing, then our fellow citizens will be more likely to realize this and seek God and so God will be glorified. As we glorify God, our lives will flourish and those around us will find our faith plausible. The loop becomes endless, repeating indefinitely because, to use computer programming terminology again, there is no 'terminating condition'.

A small town near Manchester, UK

Sunday lunch was always a high point of the week for Tom and Jane. Ever since the kids were small, Tom had enjoyed sitting down to the Sunday roast. The nest had been empty for some years but they saw no need to innovate now. Jane always got the meal ready before going to the service. The menu was always the same: roast beef, roast potatoes, peas and carrots followed by a delicious crumble. Jane set the oven timer and the smell that greeted them when they got home from the morning service was out of this world. Tom and Jane often invited friends from church to come back with them to share the meal but today they were on their own. Because it was almost their wedding anniversary, Tom opened a bottle of wine (French wine of course!) that he had been saving for the occasion.

As they sipped their cups of coffee, feeling rather replete, Jane rather surprised Tom. 'I've been wondering about something all through the meal. At breakfast we were saying that we find it difficult at church when nothing changes. Week after week the same songs, the same Bible texts – it's just too predictable. And then what do we do? We come home and have the same Sunday lunch that we've been enjoying for the past thirty years. Is there something wrong with us? Aren't we being a bit hypocritical?'

Tom felt a wave of irritation. He liked to think that he was a logical person, always trying to be consistent in his thinking. But Jane had a knack for putting her finger on his contradictions and his first response could sometimes be curt. Today was different. Their breakfast conversation had opened the communication channels between them about their church commitment and, for once, he managed to control his irritation and ask his wife if she thought that they were demanding too much of their church.

Jane's answer surprised him for the second time. 'Recently, I've been listening to a preacher from London on the internet. He has a weekly podcast and I put it on while I'm doing the ironing. Last week, he was talking about the letters to the seven churches at the beginning of Revelation and he talked about a thing he called "revitalisation".'

'Never heard of it,' was Tom's response, as if it was jargon that he could dismiss. He was slightly allergic to anything that he thought came from America.

'Just wait a second', was Jane's calm reply, 'and hear me out. This preacher was saying that churches have to repent just like men and women have to. Because "repent" just means accepting that your way of thinking is all wrong and that you have to change your mind. Just like when you become a Christian.'

'Go on,' said Tom, not quite seeing where this was going.

'Well, he spoke about Revelation 2 and the church in Ephesus, and pointed out that they had forsaken their first love so they had to do three things: remember from where they had fallen, repent and do the things that they did at first.'

'Ah,' said Tom, as he suddenly grasped what Jane was saying. 'That means that even in the early days of the church, the believers could drop into a routine and go through the motions as I was saying at breakfast. So the Bible recognizes the danger and even says that change is possible. Wow! That's encouraging.'

'Exactly!' Jane answered. 'But it also means that we don't have to reject the past and all the good things that have happened in the church over the years! And by the way, I've been thinking. Why don't we have a curry for lunch next Sunday for a change?'

A city in the west of France

Twice a month, Guillaume and Valérie spent Sunday lunchtime with their families, a longstanding tradition in France. This week it was the turn of Guillaume's parents, who lived about thirty kilometres away. After church, the young couple made the drive knowing exactly what awaited them: a splendid meal and much reminiscing about the good old days. The Marchal seniors lived in a small but comfortable home on a quiet road. The furnishing was classically French – no flat-pack furniture in their home!

Guillaume and Valérie settled down in the living room for the habitual aperitif. Guillaume often chose the Pineau des Charentes from the Cognac region of France, but Valérie stuck to fruit juice because she always drove home after their visit to Guillaume's parents. Thirty minutes later, they sat down at the dining room table knowing that the four course meal would last at least two hours. Guillaume's mother had prepared asparagus with balsamic vinegar as a starter, followed by beef bourguignon and carrots washed down with a red wine from Bordeaux. Guillaume's father always joked that Bordeaux wine was mentioned in the Bible because at the wedding at Cana they saved 'the best wine' for last. On the cheeseboard, there was a plentiful variety of local produce and the meal finished with an apple tart made from a recipe handed down from Guillaume's grandmother, who came from Normandy.

Over coffee, Guillaume's father launched into his favourite subject: nostalgia. 'When I was sixteen, I had to start work as an apprentice. I had to cycle to the factory, whatever the weather, and the work was tough. I had to stand up all day at the lathe and it was hot and dusty. The wages were low and the foreman was demanding. But – and here's the thing – we were happy with what we had! I remember buying my first portable cassette player. I used to go jogging with my friends and we thought it marvellous to be able to listen to music while we were running. But it's not like today. When we had had enough exercise, we used to go to one of our homes and chat for hours. Of course we didn't have mobile phones to look at every few seconds so we just enjoyed each other's company. We never missed our youth group on Saturday evenings and we always attended the Sunday service.'

Guillaume listened to his father fondly. He could have been irritated listening to these memories but he had had a nice meal and he found it amusing that, despite his seeming preference for the spartan conditions of the past, his father had gradually made his home very comfortable. He even had a smart-phone. The reality was that, like everyone else, his parents did enjoy today's luxuries. Guillaume had once read that even the lowliest council flat was more comfortable than King Louis XIV's palace in Versailles.

But there was a price to pay. Even his parents were not as 'committed' (to use their pastor's expression) as they used to be. Guillaume couldn't put his finger on why he thought that, but the slightest cough seemed to be a reason for them to stay at home, and they seemed to spend a lot of time and money on holidays in the sun.

He remembered that morning's sermon. The pastor had preached on some verses from the first chapter of Haggai:

> This is what the Lord Almighty says: 'These people say, "The time has not yet come to rebuild the Lord's house."' Then the word of the Lord came through the prophet Haggai: 'Is it a time for you yourselves to be living in your panelled houses, while this house remains a ruin?'
> (Haggai 1:2–4)

The pastor had finished with some words of Haggai's contemporary, Zechariah: '"Return to me," declares the Lord Almighty, "and I will return to you"' (Zechariah 1:3).

Guillaume began to see that the consumer mentality of today's Western society can easily become prevalent among Christians too. And, if he was honest, it was probably true when it came to Valérie and himself. Ultimately, there was no way to bring new life to a church other than to listen to the Bible's main message, repeated over and over again: 'Put God first.'

Guillaume realized that there were a lot of things he wanted to discuss with Valérie as they drove home.

A village in central Romania

By Sunday lunch, the whole family was starving. Three hours spent at church after breakfast was the weekly routine. At nine o'clock, there was the church prayer meeting, during which Stefan had to give a short sermon. An hour later, there was the church Bible study, mainly consisting of teaching from Stefan. Then at eleven o'clock, there was the service with hymn singing and a sermon, where it was Stefan's responsibility to both lead worship and preach.

As they laid the table before the midday meal, Ana smiled and said to Stefan with a touch of irony, 'I hope you're enjoying your day of rest, my love.'

They always enjoyed the feast that Ana prepared for the family every Sunday. Today it was *sarmale* (cabbage rolls) and polenta served with sour cream and Romanian cheese. As a special treat, Ana had made some *papanași*, a cottage cheese and semolina mixture covered in cream and blueberry jam – delicious, but rather filling.

To help with their digestion, Stefan and Ana went for a walk in the countryside while the boys met up with their friends to play football at the village playing field. They needed to use up their energy after sitting still all morning. Like all young people, they were used to surfing the internet and, if something didn't interest them, they would move on quickly. Three hours sitting in the same place in church was hard for them as teenagers.

As Stefan and Ana walked along the riverbank, their thoughts turned back to their breakfast conversation.

'Wasn't it great to see Elena at the service this morning?' Ana began. 'I can't remember the last time a teenage girl came to our church of her own free will, without her parents. In fact, I think her parents are Orthodox and not very practising either.'

'I wonder what she thought of it,' mused Stefan.

'And I wonder what the church members thought of her!' was Ana's immediate response. 'Wearing jeans to church! Wearing make-up! And with her head uncovered during the times of prayer!'

Stefan's response was more measured. 'Oh, I think our church members want to see people understand the gospel and come to Christ. The real problem emerges after they make that decision. We seem to have so many rules to obey to be a good enough Christian to become a church member.'

'It's strange,' added Ana. 'We say we are based on the Bible in all matters of belief and behaviour. But other things have crept in that seem to be more important. Perhaps because they're so visible and easy to impose on others.'

Stefan reached for the pocket New Testament he always carried with him. 'Exactly, my love. It may be just a coincidence, but I was reading Paul's letter to the Colossians only yesterday, and I fell on this verse.' He thumbed through the well-worn little volume and read aloud:

> Since you died with Christ to the elemental spiritual forces of this world, why, as though you still belonged to the world, do you submit to its rules: 'Do not handle! Do not taste! Do not touch!'? These rules, which have to do with things that are all destined to perish with use, are based on merely human commands and teachings.
> (Colossians 2:20–22)

Ana's face showed her surprise that the Bible spoke so clearly about what she had come to call legalism, though she wouldn't have dared use the word to her Christian friends in the village.

'And what is even more extraordinary', Stefan went on, 'is the next verse. "Such regulations indeed have an appearance of wisdom, with their self-imposed worship, their false humility and their harsh treatment of the body, but they lack any value in restraining sensual indulgence" (Colossians 2:23). Did you hear that, Ana? Such rules don't help us progress spiritually. I think that we're going to have to work on this in our church. Although I don't see how for the moment.'

Ana encouraged him. 'I'm sure we'll find a way, my darling. The Lord will help us.'

3

Is revitalisation biblical?

I am an evangelical Christian and I try to develop my thoughts and actions according to biblical teaching. I must admit that I am surprised at the flimsy interpretations I sometimes hear from some preachers and fellow Christians. So what is the biblical basis of revitalisation?

I have come to the conclusion that the concept of revitalisation runs right through the Bible, starting from the Old Testament. The apostle Paul writes, 'Everything that was written in the past was written to teach us, so that through the endurance taught in the Scriptures and the encouragement they provide we might have hope' (Romans 15:4). The story of God's people in the Old Testament has many parallels with church life today. The church (the people of God of the new covenant) has many privileges in comparison with the people of Israel before the coming of Christ (for example, the fullness of Scripture and the Holy Spirit poured out on every believer) but there is much that we can learn and apply about revitalisation from the Old Testament.

Revitalisation in the Old Testament

Let's think about the big picture. After sin came into the world and cut humans off from God, he revealed himself more and more clearly over the years. He first developed a relationship with the patriarchs. They trusted God even though they did not have a great deal of knowledge of who he was: 'Abram believed the LORD, and he credited it to him as righteousness' (Genesis 15:6). However, Abraham did not yet have a complete understanding of God's character. Many years later, God used Moses as the channel to communicate this framework of holiness to the people of Israel (the Ten Commandments) and the way of forgiveness through the sacrificial system. The act of circumcision was a sign of belonging to the covenant people.

Here is where we reach the need for revitalisation. Outward signs of belonging were not enough. The people of Israel put their trust too often in these things alone. The role of the prophets was to point to inward trust and obedience rather than going through the motions of doing visible things but not doing them from the heart.

> This is what the LORD Almighty, the God of Israel, says: Reform your ways and your actions, and I will let you live in this place. Do not trust in deceptive words and say, 'This is the temple of the LORD, the temple of the LORD, the temple of the LORD!'
> (Jeremiah 7:3–4)

> 'When you offer blind animals for sacrifice, is that not wrong? When you sacrifice lame or diseased animals, is that not wrong? Try offering them to your governor! Would he be pleased with you? Would he accept you?' says the LORD Almighty.
> (Malachi 1:8)

> When will the New Moon be over
>   that we may sell grain,
> and the Sabbath be ended
>   that we may market wheat?
> (Amos 8:5)

The prophets were very conscious that, even in the time of Moses, God was aware of this danger: 'Circumcise your hearts, therefore, and do not be stiff-necked any longer' (Deuteronomy 10:16). Jeremiah insists on the need to circumcise not just the flesh but also the heart (see Jeremiah 4:4, 9:25). Ezekiel proclaims that God will take away their heart of stone and give them a heart of flesh (see Ezekiel 11:19; 36:26). This is followed by the vision of the valley of dry bones, a very eloquent picture of revitalisation. I am sure that many Christians over the years have looked at their church and repeated the question, 'Can these bones live?' (Ezekiel 37:3). Fortunately, the story ends with the promise of God: 'I will put my Spirit in you and you will live' (Ezekiel 37:14).

Another clue in the Old Testament that helps us to understand why revitalisation is needed is the repeated cycle of events. A key verse can be found in Judges: 'After that whole generation had been gathered to their ancestors, another generation grew up who knew neither the LORD nor what he had done for Israel' (Judges 2:10). This underlines how important (and how difficult) it can be to pass the baton to the next generation. This pattern can be seen in the cycle of kings recounted in the books of Kings and Chronicles. A good king is often followed by several kings who do not have the same commitment to the God of Israel and who allow idolatry and injustice to creep in and be accepted. But God – how reassuring those two words are – calls a prophet to denounce the evil and a king responds by doing away with idol worship in the high places and re-establishing heartfelt worship in the sanctuary in Jerusalem. Manassah, one of the worst kings in the history of Israel, was soon followed by Josiah, who renewed Israel's covenant with God (see 2 Kings 21 – 23).

Another interesting approach is to read how God revitalised his people after their return from exile. The southern kingdom had been deported to Babylon in order to bring them to repentance, that is, a change of heart and of thinking. They had learnt their lesson and idolatry was no longer a burning issue. When Babylon was conquered by Persia, the new regime allowed the Jews to return to Jerusalem but that was where the hard work began, as we read in the books of Ezra and Nehemiah. The leaders faced opposition both from the outside and from within.

The first return to rebuild the temple of Jerusalem was under the leadership of Zerubbabel the governor and Jeshua the high priest in 537 BC. However, after a few years, 'the work on the house of God in Jerusalem came to a standstill' (Ezra 4:24). In 520 BC, two prophets then came onto the scene to revitalise the work: 'Now Haggai the prophet and Zechariah the prophet, a descendant of Iddo, prophesied to the Jews in Judah and Jerusalem in the name of the God of Israel' (Ezra 5:1). They had two very different personalities but the Lord used them both to encourage the people to finish building the temple of Jerusalem. Haggai was a very practical man and put his finger on the problem: 'The word of the LORD came through the prophet Haggai: "Is it a time for you yourselves to be living in your panelled houses, while this house remains a ruin?"' (Haggai 1:3–4). Personal comfort had become the priority and it had been put higher on the agenda than serving the Lord. Haggai passed on to the people the message that God was calling them to give careful thought to their ways (Haggai 1:5, 7) but he also reminded them of God's promise, 'I am with you' (Haggai 1:13). Some of Zechariah's prophecies are much more complex but the opening verses make the fundamental message very clear: 'This is what the LORD Almighty says: "Return to me," declares the LORD Almighty, "and I will return to you"' (Zechariah 1:3).

As well as dealing with the wrong priorities of God's people, Zerubbabel and Jeshua also had to deal with opposition from outside. There was the temptation to compromise when some of the enemies of Judah and Benjamin offered their help in rebuilding the temple because, 'like you, we seek your God' (Ezra 4:2). When this offer was refused, these enemies 'set out to discourage the people of Judah and make them afraid to go on building. They bribed officials to work against them and frustrate their plans' (Ezra 4:4–5). In the end, they succeeded in putting an end to the work by writing to the king of Persia accusing the Jews of being rebellious and refusing to pay their taxes. The king sent a letter ordering the work to stop. It was at that point that Haggai and Zechariah prophesied and the people set to work again in spite of the letter.

Revitalisation is never a one-off event. It must be an ongoing process. Almost eighty years later, in 458 BC, Ezra led a huge delegation back to Jerusalem because a new problem had arisen. The account is in Ezra 7 – 10. Around that time, the prophet Malachi had denounced the half-hearted attitude of the inhabitants of Jerusalem: 'A son honours his father, and a slave his master. If I am a father, where is the honour due to me? If I am a master, where is the respect due to me?' (Malachi 1:6). When Ezra arrived in Jerusalem, what did he find? In a word, compromise. After the amazing way in which God had enabled them to rebuild the temple and restore God-honouring worship, just two generations down the line, the situation had deteriorated to such an extent that several leaders came to Ezra and said:

> The people of Israel, including the priests and the Levites, have not kept themselves separate from the neighbouring peoples with their detestable practices, like those of the Canaanites, Hittites, Perizzites, Jebusites, Ammonites, Moabites, Egyptians and Amorites. They have taken some of their daughters as wives for themselves and their sons, and have mingled the holy race with the peoples around them. And the leaders and officials have led the way in this unfaithfulness. (Ezra 9:1–2)

Ezra was appalled and his first reaction was to fall on his knees and pray. And then he went to work with faithful men and organized a way to look at each case individually until everyone had confessed their disobedience and separated themselves from their foreign (that is, idolatrous) wives.

A dozen years later, Nehemiah undertook the long journey to Jerusalem from Susa, in Persia, where he was the cupbearer to the king. He had heard reports that the wall of Jerusalem was broken down and that the gates burned with fire, which left the city vulnerable to attacks. His wise but vigorous way of working is a great example to anyone involved in church revitalisation today. We read in Nehemiah 3 that he first analysed the situation by inspecting the walls by night so as to avoid opposition before he had understood the situation. Then he told the leaders how the gracious hand of God had been on him from the time he first spoke to the king in Susa and encouraged them to start rebuilding. They responded positively and began the good work despite opposition from several men, which continued with mockery – 'What they are building – even a fox climbing up on it would break down their wall of stones!' (Nehemiah 4:3) – and an attempt to discredit Nehemiah by having him hide from danger overnight in the temple, which would have been a sin for a man who wasn't a priest (see Nehemiah 6). Nehemiah encouraged everyone from the leaders down to the ordinary citizens to become involved. At times, the fear of attack forced them to build with one hand while holding a weapon in the other. They were organized in teams, they worked from sunrise to sunset and they got the job done in just fifty-two days (see Nehemiah 4; 6:15). Even so, Nehemiah had to deal with some internal problems. For example, some people were selfishly exploiting the situation in order to increase their wealth (see Nehemiah 5). Nehemiah acted vigorously to put an end to this and led by example. Even though he could have received the food allotted to the governor, he paid out of his own pocket to feed the 150 officials who ate at his table every day.

Revitalisation in the New Testament

When we turn to the New Testament, we are struck by the contrast between the exciting teaching of Jesus and the difficulty that the early churches had in putting it into practice. Several of Paul's letters were sent to churches to try to work out their difficulties. It reminds me of a joke I heard once. Two Christian friends who hadn't seen each other for some time happened to meet one day. The first one said, 'I've joined a church like the ones in the New Testament.' His friend replied, 'Yes, we've got lots of problems in our church too!'

Despite the real changes that Christ brings into a person's life, the process of sanctification will not be completed on this side of eternity. Churches are composed of not-yet-sanctified Christians. That is why revitalisation is an ongoing process. If a church does not progress, then it will probably start to regress, like every one of us in our Christian lives.

Revelation 2 – 3 is a very significant part of the New Testament for our subject. Since seven is the symbolic number for completeness, I think that the seven churches represent all the churches in the world, in every nation and every age from the time of the apostles until the present day because the same difficulties and temptations have faced all Christians and every church throughout time. This is confirmed by the end of each letter in Revelation 2 – 3 where we read the words, 'Whoever has ears, let them hear what the Spirit says to the churches.' Each of the messages should be listened to by the churches, in the plural.

Each of the seven letters in Revelation starts in the same way: 'These are the words of him who' with several references to the vision of Jesus in Revelation 1. We could say that these seven messages are 'what Jesus thinks' of these churches:

- Ephesus and Laodicea are in grave danger (churches 1 and 7).
- Smyrna (church 2) and Philadelphia (church 6) are doing fine but they are still encouraged to progress. 'I know your afflictions . . . do not be afraid' (Revelation 2:9–10) for Smyrna and 'I have placed before you an open door that no one can shut' (Revelation 3:8) for Philadelphia.
- The three churches in the middle, Pergamum, Thyatira and Sardis (churches 3, 4 and 5), are average – we might say passable – but they must avoid self-satisfaction and act on areas of danger.

So what are the problems in five of these churches? There is a whole range, which we can easily identify with today:

- Ephesus: the loss of their first love (see Revelation 2:4).
- Pergamum: the need to fight against error and idolatry, which leads to immorality (see Revelation 2:14–15).

35

- Thyatira: the need to fight against sin and sexual immorality by not tolerating 'inspired teachers', in this case the prophetess Jezebel (see Revelation 2:20).
- Sardis: the church has a reputation for being alive but it is dead. Outwardly, everything looks good but their deeds are not complete in the sight of God (see Revelation 3:1–2).
- Laodicea: the church is lukewarm. Hot water is useful and cold water is refreshing but lukewarm water is no good at all (see Revelation 3:15).

In the message to each of the churches, the same verb is used: repent. The root of this word means changing the way that you think. This has immediate consequences for the way that we behave. To become a Christian, we have to repent (that is, recognize that what we thought was the normal way of life is wrong) and believe. As believers, we need to repent and confess our sins to stay in close fellowship with God. The first of Luther's *Ninety-Five Theses* states that, 'When our Lord and Master Jesus Christ said, "Repent" (Matthew 4:17), he willed the entire life of believers to be one of repentance.' That is true of us collectively as well as individually, and that means that churches may be called to repentance.

We can see this pattern emerging when we look more closely at two of the churches.

Ephesus (Revelation 2:5)

- Remember the height from which you have fallen
- Repent
- Do the things you did at first

Sardis (Revelation 3:2–3)

- Wake up and strengthen what remains and is about to die
- Remember what you have received and heard
- Obey it and repent

As we reach the end of this chapter, I think that we can say that, without a doubt, revitalisation is a truly scriptural concept. The Bible shows us that revitalisation involves both human action in the form of repentance, and God's response, which is to breathe new life by his Spirit when the church hears what the Spirit is saying.

A small town near Manchester, UK

Jane picked up the remote and turned off the television with a tut.

'I'm fed up with these politicians. All they ever do is criticize each other. It's so easy to find fault with others but a bit more difficult to do something.'

Tom was in a slightly more jovial mood and tried to calm his wife down without contradicting her. 'That reminds me of a good joke I heard at work last week,' he said. 'Whatever did Adam and Eve find to talk about in the garden of Eden since there was no one else there to criticize!'

'OK, Tom, you're right. But what happened last week in my tutor group at school has been running through my head for the past few days. You know that every Friday I meet with my group to talk about school life and all I ever hear is complaints – about the timetable, about the school meals, about the amount of homework. So last Friday I finally said, "So what do you suggest?" and the result was dead silence. None of the pupils could find a single positive idea to put forward!'

'It doesn't surprise me, Jane. I've been wondering if I'm guilty of the same thing about our church. I know what I don't like, but what do I want things to be like in today's world? We can't turn the clock back to when we were younger. It was a different world. Our town was different then. There was more respect for Christian values. There was no internet, no social media . . . '

'True, but we used to moan about the hours people spent in front of the television. We used to laugh about people getting square eyes!'

'Sure, we mustn't idealize the past. That sort of sentimentality won't help us at all. Even nostalgia isn't what it used to be, as they say!'

'Oh, Tom. What's got into you this evening?'

'I don't know. It's just that when you shared with me that church revitalisation is a biblical concept, it was like a weight falling off my shoulders and I began to think about the changes that could be made at our church. I started to imagine what I wanted to happen. And, believe it or not, I started to have some practical ideas!'

'I'm all ears,' Jane exclaimed.

'OK. Here are some of the thoughts I had when I started to look at the beginning of the book of Acts in my daily Bible reading. The early Christians were committed to fellowship and that included meals together, learning from the apostles' teaching and prayer. Couldn't we aim for that for a start?'

'Sounds good,' said Jane. 'So what do you suggest practically?'

'Well, we could encourage people to talk to each other, and what better way to do that than around meal tables? And we could start a prayer meeting for the church and for our town. Then we could encourage more creativity in the way that we teach God's Word. There are loads of things on the internet about this.'

Jane's response was a bit downbeat. 'You don't think that you'll do that all on your own, do you?'

'Ah,' replied Tom, 'There's something else. I've been looking at our denomination's website and I've discovered several ministries that could get alongside a local church like ours to help us think through the issues and make positive changes. I just didn't know that all of this was happening around us.'

Jane couldn't help joining in his merriment. 'You sound like a modern John Newton, Tom. "I once was blind but now I see!"'

A city in the west of France

It was time to leave Guillaume's parents after the Sunday meal. After some final farewells, the young couple got into their new hybrid car. Like many people today, they were very ecologically minded. They tried to buy organic food, they recycled as much as possible, and so a more environmentally friendly car was an obvious choice. But Guillaume did have a pang of conscience about one of their favourite leisure activities.

'Valérie, I've been thinking,' he started hesitantly as she drove the car out of his parents' street. 'We like travelling to other countries, but aren't we contributing to global warming by flying to those places?'

Valérie admitted to herself that there was some truth in this question, though she was also aware of the danger of a new environmental legalism.

'You're right, my love,' she said. 'But we enjoy seeing other cultures and appreciating the diversity of our world.'

Guillaume smiled as he remembered their trips abroad. 'I suppose so. Just think of all the things that we would've missed if we hadn't taken those short breaks. We wouldn't have known that in Norway they have their main meal of the day at four o'clock in the afternoon. We were so hungry by that time.'

'Just like we were in Spain waiting for the evening meal at ten o'clock at night,' added Valérie.

Their conversation wandered around all the cultural differences they had seen in the world, some of them bringing them to fits of laughter.

'Do you remember when we were in the USA last summer?' asked Guillaume. 'We wanted to cross the road and the sign said, "Don't walk," so we ran across! That was so French!'

But after a while, they sobered down and Guillaume recalled the question that he had been thinking about: how can we truly put God first in our lives today? He asked Valérie what she thought as he had grown to value her insights.

She was silent for a few moments before wondering aloud if there was a link between that question and their previous discussion about other cultures. 'Putting God first isn't an abstract thing. It's living in our own culture. It's being authentic with God in the world we live in.'

'Exactly,' agreed Guillaume. 'We're trying to live as disciples of Jesus and that's why we believe in creation care.'

'And that's why Wycliffe Bible Translators are trying to make the Bible available in every language. How can you put God first if you have to build a relationship with him without using your mother tongue?' Valérie was warming up. 'And that's why I went to that training day last year about ethnodoxology. Do you remember? It was all about using the musical traditions of every people to worship God in a way that resonates deeply with their cultural context.'

'So,' mused Guillaume, 'putting God first means seeing his relevance – if that isn't too weak a word – in every area of our lives. And that has implications for our church! When we meet together, we need to learn how to live for God in today's world and not hide behind our usual patterns of worship. I must admit that I'm a bit fed up with hearing that such and such a thing is "the way that we've always done it".'

'Oh, Guillaume. You'll never change, will you? But I love you for your passion.'

A village in central Romania

Once a year, Stefan and Ana were invited to spend a few days with their friends, Gheorghe and Maria, in the Carpathian mountains. Stefan and Gheorghe had been students together at the seminary in Bucharest. Their friendship had grown over the years and their wives got on well too. It was always a great pleasure to spend a few days in the log cabin that belonged to Gheorghe's family. The twins had gone by train to Bucharest to stay with their grandparents and discover the big city.

After leaving their cars at a small parking place, Stefan, Ana and their friends still had several hundred metres to climb through the forest carrying everything that they needed for the stay, including the food.

For the first evening, Ana had brought a thick soup and Maria had made a huge cheese pie. As they sipped herbal tea after the meal, Gheorghe said, 'Every time I come here I think of that joke – what's the difference between a pastor and an evangelist? Do you know it?'

Stefan and Ana shook their heads and Stefan said, 'Go on. You're dying to tell us.'

Gheorghe launched in, 'A pastor and an evangelist decided to spend a few days hunting bears in the mountains. On the first morning, the evangelist set out straight after breakfast but the pastor said he would first spend some time in prayer and the word. Half an hour later, the pastor heard loud cries, looked out the window and saw the evangelist racing down the slope towards the cabin, closely followed by a bear. In a flash, the pastor opened the door and prayed that the evangelist would be far enough ahead of the pursuing bear to get into the cabin so that he could slam the door shut and keep the bear out. But at the last moment, the evangelist veered to one side, the bear came into the cabin and the evangelist shouted, "It's your turn! It's up to you to deal with him now. I'm off to find another one."'

They all roared with laughter and told each other more jokes that they had heard recently. After a while, Ana and Maria went off to bed in their rooms on the first floor. The journey had been tiring and they knew that their husbands had a lot to catch up on.

Stefan came back to the joke about the hunters and shared his concerns about the church he was pastoring. 'That joke was funny but, in our village, we aren't seeing any bears come into the church. And I'm not sure the church members would know how to relate to them if they did! We need a breath of new life but I don't know where to start or how to go about it.'

'I can sympathize with you,' Gheorghe responded. 'I was in your situation a few months ago. Then I attended the European Leadership Forum, and I no longer feel so alone. We all need people to stand with us, to coach us and counsel us. And that's what I found at ELF.'

'I'm afraid I've never heard of it. What is it?'

Gheorghe was keen to get Stefan on board. 'They hold a conference in Poland every year and there's even a Church Revitalisation Network, which is part of the reason I went last year.'

'I've heard of "revitalisation",' Stefan said. 'Didn't they organize a short seminar about this at the seminary in Bucharest last year?'

Gheorghe told his friend that he had attended it and that it had opened his eyes to all sorts of possibilities. 'That's why I signed up for ELF.'

'I don't think I can afford to go to an international conference like that,' Stefan admitted.

'But that's the great thing. They have scholarships for people from Romania because our currency is weak. And there's something else too. You can also sign up to a year-round mentoring scheme via video meetings. I'm in a group this year with pastors from across Europe and I'm learning so much. It's a real support for me in my ministry.'

The next morning, Stefan slept in and woke up feeling refreshed and more encouraged – though he had had a strange dream of being in a webinar with a group of bears discussing how to make a good cheese pie.

4

What should a healthy church look like?

At the end of chapter 3, we talked about repentance. Fundamentally changing the way that we think has immediate consequences on what we do and how we behave. But you might respond with a question: 'On what criteria should we evaluate a church and ask what it should look like so that we can "repent" and bring about change?'

On one level, there is no easy answer because there is no template for what a church should look like. A church in Geneva at the time of the Reformation would not have looked like a church in a student area of a big city today, or a church in a Muslim majority country, or a church in a village of hunter-gatherers in the equatorial rainforests of Africa. A church in a rural community may look very different from an urban church and a church in a nation with a long history of Christianity will be influenced strongly by what has happened in the past, a very different situation from a village in Papua New Guinea where the gospel is being received for the first time. Last but not least, our experience of living our church life in the periods of lockdown during the Covid-19 pandemic has also influenced our concept of church.

Here are some thoughts about the early church. In Acts 2:42–47, we catch a glimpse of the health of the early church. All too soon, this health was under pressure as the church grew, prompting Paul to write to the churches (sometimes with harsh words) as they allowed tradition to have a negative impact on the church. So what does a healthy church look like in the twenty-first century? Is it a matter of size, the make-up of the church, or its location? Is it about the age range of the congregation? Is it dependent on the style of worship, the version of the Bible a church uses or even whether they have a full-time pastor? While all of these may be significant, they do not make a healthy church.

In the early church, the Christians were devoted to prayer, teaching, fellowship and the breaking of bread, which resulted in people being saved and disciples being built up in the faith. A healthy church is defined by these things. Healthy churches pray together, take God's Word seriously and seek to live by it. Fellowship is real, leading people to share each other's lives in a variety of ways. Reaching out with the love of Jesus, sharing faith and seeing people saved are all signs of a healthy church.[1]

One of the basic problems was – and still is – that 'they allowed tradition to have a negative impact on the church.' Let's imagine a man who knows nothing about Christianity. He is stranded on a desert island after a shipwreck and finds a copy of the New Testament. He reads it, believes and puts his trust in Jesus. While waiting to be rescued, he imagines joining a church back in the West. Would he be surprised at what he finds when he comes back to his home country? Would he expect to find churches such as those we have today? Of course there may be good reasons why church life and organization has developed as it has but, nevertheless, I think that we should take these questions seriously.

I think that a good place to start thinking through these questions is to ask, 'What are the minimum criteria of a local church?' I have drawn up the following points, which I use when teaching revitalisation in Bible schools or local churches. I have found that there is a real consensus that this is a fair summary of what the Bible says about a local church.

A local church is a group of Christians who:

- meet together (see Acts 2:42) to devote themselves to the apostles' teaching (i.e., the teaching of the word), fellowship in a spirit of solidarity, the breaking of bread (i.e., fellowship meals, communion and worship) and prayer
- welcome all those who believe in Jesus, regardless of their age, their origins, or whether they are male or female (see Romans 15:7)
- meet locally (see 1 Corinthians 1:2; Galatians 1:2; Ephesians 1:1; Philemon 1:2 etc.)
- have elders and deacons as recognized leaders (see Acts 14:23; 1 Timothy 3; Titus 1) who watch over the life of the church and serve the people

---

1 "What is a healthy church?," www.revitalisation.fr/en/issues/9-what-is-a-healthy-church.

- recognize that every person has and can use his or her spiritual gifts
  (see 1 Corinthians 12)
- organize baptisms (see Acts 18:8) and the Lord's Supper
  (see 1 Corinthians 11:23–24)
- have love as the distinctive sign (see John 13:35)
- are involved in society and proclaim salvation in Jesus Christ
  (see 1 Timothy 2:1–7; 1 Peter 2:9)

Of course this is the bare bones. A lot more could be said for each point. In the first point, for example, I have extended the meaning of the breaking of bread from the literal sense of fellowship meals to include taking communion (i.e., the Lord's Supper because that is where it was probably celebrated in the early church) and from there to worship because sharing in the bread and wine meant worshipping the Saviour. But when we are talking about church revitalisation, the real reason for presenting this summary lies elsewhere. If this list covers every important aspect of a local church, then anything not mentioned is not a binding matter for all churches and Christians.

Let me give you a concrete example. A few years ago, an article appeared in the magazine of the denomination that I belong to, written by a pastor who had decided to start a second service in his church because there was not room in his building to welcome any more people at the Sunday morning service. He could have decided to hold a second service at a different time on a Sunday morning but he struck out in a different direction and decided to run a Saturday evening service instead. When he referred to this in his article, several people wrote to the editor of the magazine criticizing my colleague for not observing 'the Lord's Day' but, when you look at the list of minimum criteria, there is no mention of the day on which the Christians had to meet.

In the course of my life, I have observed two very different styles of church life in Western Europe.

First, when I was a newly born-again Christian, most churches took a rather formal approach, with the men in suits and ties and the women in dresses observing silence in the sanctuary before the service started. The 'hymn sandwich' was the standard order of service, with an organ (or harmonium) for the music. Most of the meetings were held on the church premises and led by the minister. I have the impression that this type of church atmosphere was predominant until the early seventies, though it can still be found today in some more traditional churches.

Later, this was followed by a more informal type of worship and church life in general. 'Californian-hippy-inspired praise music' became the main aspect of Sunday services, often led by a worship leader with a guitar, though a wider range of instruments were included as the years went by. Casual clothing became the norm because church attendance was seen as an optional leisure activity – people wore formal clothing to go to work but not at weekends. Group leadership developed as the preferred style of church structure (which was more biblical) and a considerable number of small groups led by laypeople developed, often in people's homes.

When it comes to revitalisation, should our aim be to use one of these two styles as a model to work towards or should we be going down a new path? In the UK, the 2004 Mission-Shaped Church report by the Church of England focused on creative 'fresh expressions' of church, leading to the interdenominational Fresh Expressions movement to promote new approaches to church.[2] I approve the motivation behind the movement and there are some interesting examples of new models of church to consider. However, much care and discernment needs to be taken to find approaches that will connect with people in your church's specific environment, especially across different European cultural contexts.

But why should we be looking for new ways to live out our church life at all? I think that it is probably because of a common factor between the two styles that I have described. Both of them can, inadvertently, lead believers to live in a sort of bubble. In the first style, people begin to think that you can be more spiritual in a place of worship than in the world outside. The same bubble effect can be produced by the second style through the emotional side of praise music, when people feel closer to God as they listen to certain styles of music. One of the important objectives of church revitalisation is to *reduce* the distance between the church and the world not by changing our theology but by preparing believers to live in the world without being of it, as Jesus said in John 17. As someone once said to me, 'The boat must be in the water but the water must not be in the boat!'

---

2 Graham Cray, *Mission-Shaped Church: Church Planting and Fresh Expressions of Church in a Changing Context* (London: Church House Publishing, 2004).

This brings us back to my very simple definition of a healthy church:

A healthy church is a fellowship of believers, redeemed through the gospel, who are learning to love God with all their heart, with all their soul, with all their mind, with all their strength (Mark 12:30), and to love people (Mark 12:31) in their cultural context.

This is where we will head as we start to look at the process of revitalisation in the next section. What would this look like in practice? What is the conceptual framework of a healthy church in today's world? And how can we make that model accessible and understandable to every church member as the environment in which revitalisation can take place?

The following infographic gives an overview of the vision of a healthy church. It is a tool that the church leaders can use and that everyone can grasp and remember.[3] Leaders can keep referring back to this pattern as they work with the members to implement changes in the church. Everyone needs to bear this big picture continually in mind in order to understand the reasons for these changes.

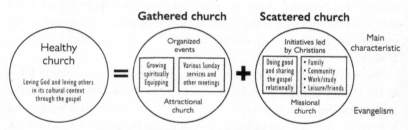

Figure 2 **Diagram of a healthy church**

Just as a hybrid car uses both petrol and electricity, this diagram illustrates the concept of a church functioning in two hybrid and complementary ways: as the gathered church and as the scattered church.[4] Through the various meetings – which are organized as events open to the church members and to the general public – the gathered church builds up believers in their faith in order to help them live as salt and light all through the week. This can sometimes attract non-Christians. However,

---

3 You can download this diagram at www.revitalisation.fr/en/strategy.
4 For further reading on this subject, I recommend Neil Hudson, *Scattered and Gathered: Equipping Disciples for the Frontline* (London: IVP, 2019).

the scattered church is intentionally missional because the believers are sent out to do good and to communicate the gospel in their daily lives.

The gathered church

The gathered church expresses that we are 'one body' in Christ and belong to one another as believers (Romans 12:5; 1 Corinthians 12:2). The goal of the gathered church is to edify (meaning build up) the lives of Christians. The role of the leaders is to 'equip God's people for works of service, so that the body of Christ may be built up' (Ephesians 4:11–12). The leaders can use all manner of activities to build up church members in the faith and to train them in practical ways to live out their lives in God's service.

One way of doing this, which is mentioned in the healthy church diagram above, is that the gathered church may offer more than one type of worship service.

The church's main Sunday service will probably retain a fairly conventional format (i.e., singing, Bible readings, prayer, the Lord's Supper and preaching). This is often the most visible 'flagship' activity of the church. It is where the preaching of the word and the sacraments, which are the 'ordinary means of grace' in God's economy, will be found week in week out. However, few non-believers will be attracted *directly* to coming to church services without some prior contact with the church or its members. We need to help to bridge this gap to introduce people to the gospel and to Christian things. One way to do this is to offer some form of alternative worship.

Alongside this primary service, there may well be an increasing number of more 'radical' targeted formats. The hope is that members of the church will find it easier to invite their non-Christian friends to these services. We can plan the approaches according to the target groups. The services may be on different days and at different times and they may have different emphases according to different approaches to spirituality or the type of people we are trying to reach (for example, the young professionals on a Sunday evening in Paris). I think that this is partly what the apostle Paul meant by being like a Jew with the Jews and being weak with the weak (see 1 Corinthians 9:19–23) but we need to think about what this involves in the reality of the cultural context of the twenty-first century. Different personalities and contrasting lifestyles make it impossible to maintain the 'one-size-fits-all' approach.

But there is also more to church than the worship services. First and foremost, there are various types of meetings primarily for believers (for example, prayer meetings, training sessions, house groups and scheduled discipleship), though it is not a problem if non-Christians are also present. Along with the times of worship, these meetings are fundamental for ensuring that discipleship takes place in the three main areas we have discussed: the social, the societal and the spiritual. The gathered church is a place where Christians can worship together and be strengthened in the faith. During the Covid-19 pandemic, we began to see that the church could gather in different ways. Some people have even stated that the future will not be a church with some internet presence but an online community with some face-to-face meetings. Only time will tell, but this does not change the general process of revitalisation described in this book.

To put all of this in concrete terms, the activities of the gathered church are generally public events listed on the church calendar and on its website. They make the church visible in the surrounding community, make it possible to forge links with the civil authorities and allow us to engage in dialogue with other organizations and religions.

It is important to notice that all of these events and activities are *attractional*. In fact, there may even be activities that are specifically designed to reach out to people outside the church. The church premises may be used in the social area (for example, for a food bank, for Alcoholics Anonymous meetings or for financial counselling) or in the cultural area (for example, the church may organize concerts or talks about art or history as a way of approaching and explaining the biblical world view).

'Attractional' implies that non-Christians will come to the church building or to church activities. There's no problem with that but, in today's world, very few people do unless they have been invited by a church member. The first contact with a Christian is usually not via the gathered church but in the course of daily life, which brings us to the scattered church.

The scattered church

When it comes to evangelism, the gathered church's characteristic is to be attractional. The scattered church provides the necessary counterpart by being *missional*. The word implies being sent. As the congregation leaves the church building, they could imagine a notice on the door saying, 'Warning! You are now entering your mission field!'

The scattered church is where we live out the four relational networks that most of us have: our family, our workplace or place of education, our leisure activities and friendships, and the wider community. Our aim in these relationships is to love others, to do good and to share the gospel when we can. That is why the missional aspect of the church is sometimes called 'incarnational': just as Jesus took on a human body and became visible, Christians become visible (and make God visible, in a sense) by their practical love for others.

The emphasis is on the initiative taken by Christians. This will often include unstructured activities outside the church walls involving church members either individually or in small groups. These activities are not found on the church calendar and they are not official public events set up by the church. But they are not necessarily private either – at least not in the sense that no one knows about them. It can be useful for Christians to inform the church leaders about some of their initiatives in order to receive prayer and advice or to share certain prayer topics with the whole church.

Our Christian life must be motivated by love for our neighbours. Some members of the church will be called to engage in social or humanitarian action in non-Christian organizations, for example, by volunteering with the Red Cross, by joining an organization that offers debt advice or even by becoming involved in local government. But everyone will watch out for opportunities to glorify God in their daily life, to do good and to speak of their faith as opportunities arise.

Every Christian can pray that God will bring us into contact with people to love and help and to whom we can witness. We can pray that these relationships will continue until these people are converted. There are several ways to do this:

- take up a hobby or join a group that brings you into contact with non-Christians on a regular basis
- connect with people online through discussion groups, making a podcast, running an online book group or another social initiative that relates to your interests
- meet non-Christians for coffee
- show hospitality towards Christians and non-Christians

Sometimes a relationship can lead to sharing our faith more intentionally:

- invite parents with their children to watch a Christian film for children or for a special Christmas or Easter event – parents may be happier to be with their children in the home of a family they know than to let them go to a church Bible club
- read the Bible in pairs or in a small group with a non-Christian

This conception of the scattered church is very relevant in the contemporary context of militant citizenship. People become involved in local issues in person or on social media as grass-roots activists, for example in the areas of ecology, local politics or in marketing. In the Western world today, I believe that this is the most effective (and the most biblical) way forward for evangelism. The goal is to remain friends with people while being transparent about our convictions.

I recognize that Christians might feel fearful about being open about their faith in public because Christian beliefs may be seen as oppressive. Some Christians may be apprehensive of risking their careers or their social standing (I will say more about this in chapter 15) but, for the moment, we should remember that the best response to this fear is the passion that comes from marvelling at the truths presented in the Bible. This comes especially from our time together in the gathered church as we worship God and receive stimulating teaching.

The implications of this model for leadership

I sometimes fear that the radical nature of this concept of the gathered and scattered church and the implications that flow from it may not be fully recognized by church leaders before they start out on the revitalisation process. They need to be aware at the very outset that the diagram gives equal weight to the gathered and scattered aspects of the church whereas, in reality, many churches give far more value to their visible togetherness (i.e., the church building, the meetings or the paid ministry). I am not saying that these are bad or unnecessary, but it is a question of the relative weight given to each aspect. Do we believe in the priesthood of all believers? Do we believe in every member ministry? Are we all called to be 'ministers' (i.e., servants)? It is true that some Christians have received particular gifts and callings (as we saw in Ephesians 4:11), but that does not mean that they have to do all the work. Their ministry is to 'equip the saints' (Ephesians 4:12, ESV). I might add, *equip not exhaust*. When we realize this, it changes the whole emphasis of what we do as a gathered church in our worship, teaching, praying, training and discipleship so that we are equipped to serve as the scattered church.

The average amount of time a person spends at work in his or her lifetime is approximately 90,000 hours. In 2019, the Lausanne Movement held the Global Workplace Forum in Manila because, according to Michael Oh, global executive director of the Lausanne Movement, 'the Christian's presence at work presents itself as the most natural, and at the same time most overlooked, opportunity to evangelize the world.' Oh stressed the fact that, 'The Great Commission can never be fulfilled by pastors and missionaries alone.'[5]

The workplace or the university are examples of the sphere of witness of individual Christians who need to be encouraged, trained and prayed for. It is a common experience that people are more likely to pray for the Sunday school teachers in a church during the service than for the primary school teachers who will spend their whole week with children. The background against which the songs for the service are projected is more likely to be a scene from the countryside than an office, a factory or a shopping centre, as if it was easier to be 'spiritual' away from the places where most of us spend our working weeks.

The fact is that we are called to be salt and light in society (Matthew 5:13). We must remain salty and let our light shine. One of the reasons for meeting together as a gathered church is to learn how to do that.

Individual Christians can go to places and do things that the church as a religious body cannot. Students are free to witness on their campus, whereas laws promoting secularism or university policies might prevent the church as a whole from doing so. While the church will stay neutral as far as political parties are concerned, an individual Christian can have a political commitment and the church can then pray for the member concerned. An individual Christian can have a regular commitment in a non-religious humanitarian organization, even though a church might be unable to be an official partner. The aim of the gathered church is not to just 'protect' the individual from the influences of the world, but to

---

5 You can find resources related to the Global Workplace Forum at www.lausanne.org/gwf.

prepare every Christian to go out into the world *as a Christian* without hiding their light under a bowl as Matthew 5:15 says. In the gathered church, Christians can be trained to think within a biblical framework in a way that connects with non-Christians. This implies that church leaders need to be prepared to do this.

At this point (and here I am speaking as a pastor), there is a real danger that the pastoral team will try to keep too great a degree of control over what members do as the scattered church. The default position to which years of church tradition can bring us is the idea that the important thing in a church is the faithfulness of Christians in attending meetings. But as a friend of mine said, 'Christ didn't redeem us so that we could go to a lot of meetings!' To be brutally honest, one reason for attending a lot of meetings can be the fear of spending time with non-Christians. That is understandable when fellowship with other believers is sweet but we must ask the Lord to give us a real love for those who are perishing.

A second danger for the pastoral team is to think that the local church is the only place in which believers can learn and have a ministry. In the scattered church, the individual Christian may need the support of other believers who are in the same situation as he or she is. For example, a student can join the student movement on their campus. There are a great number of what are sometimes called 'parachurch movements' (wrongly in my opinion, because they are part of the universal church with a particular calling or service which the local church cannot provide). These movements are a great help in reaching out in particular contexts. I have just mentioned universities, but we could add many other environments such as schools, hospitals, the armed forces, other religious groups, sport or the arts. However, the local church remains the place where everyone with all their differences can gather to worship and be encouraged to be disciples in the widest sense.

A third danger is to be found right at the top of the healthy church diagram. The emphasis of the scattered church is initiatives led by Christians. How far can this go? There is no single answer, but there is a possible guideline. We all know that we get on better with some people than with others. We may have a similar background or outlook on life, or maybe it is 'chemistry'. Whatever the explanation, when a contact is established, it is almost impossible to hand that person over to the care of someone else. So if a one-to-one Bible study between a church member and a non-Christian leads to that person's conversion and they find one or two others who want to learn about Jesus, this could become a regular meeting without ever being a public meeting of the church that is announced on its website. It may even be difficult for some new Christians to begin attending the public meetings of the church because of their marital situation (opposition from their spouse for example) or because their hours of work clash with church services. Let us rejoice that they can meet informally. It is a positive extension of the visible church.

A small town near Manchester, UK

Tom was a loyal fan of his local football team. You had to be loyal to support them because there were no great successes within living memory. The main aim of the club seemed to be avoiding relegation season after season but that was enough for Tom to feel the tension mounting every match day. If they couldn't win at home, then the chances of staying up were slim.

Fortunately, his best friend Martin was also a fan and they had season tickets for adjacent seats. How can you enjoy a match if you have no one to complain to about the referee's decisions or the stupidity of the manager's team selection? And of course it meant that he had someone to celebrate with when the team scored. There's a Swedish proverb that says, 'Shared joy is a double joy; shared sorrow is half a sorrow.'

Of course solidarity with your team only goes so far. Tom probably didn't realize that when he got home after the match he made a subtle distinction in telling Jane either, 'We won' or, 'They lost.' After all, it isn't the fault of the supporters if the team loses.

Today, Tom and Martin were early for the kick-off of the cup match against a team in a higher division. The teams were warming up, the away fans were already chanting and, for the next ninety minutes, the drama would be non-stop. At half-time, with the home team leading 2–1, Tom and Martin were trying to cool down with a fizzy drink.

'That's been quite a first half!' exclaimed Tom. 'Both of our goals were brilliantly taken, but can we hang on for another forty-five minutes?'

Martin looked slightly dubious and then surprised Tom. 'It's such a pity that the services at our church aren't as exciting as this match.'

Tom was speechless for a few seconds. Then he replied, 'I was sure that I was the only one who thought that way – apart from Jane, of course.'

With a wry smile, Martin explained that two other couples, the Chapmans and the Wyatts, had been thinking the same thing for some time. None of them knew what to do about their concerns.

'Why don't we all get together some time and share our thoughts?' suggested Tom. 'But we must be careful that it doesn't turn into a witch hunt, trying to find who's at fault for the state of affairs. We all are to some extent and just complaining doesn't change anything. I've had several long chats about this with Jane recently and we don't want things to become sour.'

'Exactly. I totally agree,' Martin quickly responded. 'But remember, Trevor Chapman is one of the elders and that should help to stop us being seen as an opposition movement.'

'And Roger Wyatt is a management consultant, so he must have a good idea of how to bring about change,' added Tom. 'If he can do it in a commercial company, there must be some similarities with a church. Except that we're more spiritual of course.'

'Speak for yourself!' Martin said. 'But seriously, Carol and I could have you all round for a meal next week. We could bring up our concerns and pray about it.'

'Great. Oh, the teams are coming out again. Fasten your seat belt. We could be in for an interesting ride this second half.'

A city in the west of France

Guillaume and Valérie realized that sooner or later they had to talk to their pastor about their concerns, but they wanted to avoid seeming critical and divisive. They both knew from their jobs that finding fault with the way that the boss ran things never brought about major change. Despite their relatively young age, they were both in management positions and had to deal with frequent strikes from the workforce. Strikes were part of French culture, and the competing trade unions knew that they had to appear to be militant and call regular strikes to attract membership, but both Guillaume and Valérie had seen that constructive dialogue could achieve far more in the long term.

But somehow they couldn't see how to start this dialogue, that is, until the church weekend came along. Every year, most of the church members and families went away to a retreat centre for a fairly relaxed weekend in the country, often with a visiting speaker to give some Bible teaching. One of the traditional events was the Saturday afternoon hike – or rather hikes, since the families with younger children and some of the older members chose to go on a much shorter walk than the fitter members of the congregation. So Guillaume and Valérie found themselves in a relatively small group along with Denis, their pastor. They set out after lunch and decided to climb to the top of the impressive hill that overlooked the conference centre. When they got to the top, they took out their refreshments and the pastor gave them the opportunity they were waiting for.

'There don't seem to be many of us opting for the long walk nowadays,' he bewailed.

Guillaume was quick to seize the opportunity. 'True. I've been wondering about that. Don't you think it has something to do with the demographics of the church?'

Denis wasn't sure what Guillaume was trying to say and asked him to explain what he meant.

'Well, for one thing, there are more and more children and the parents feel that they have to stay and look after them on the shorter walk,' said Guillaume. 'And there are more older people in the church too. They're still quite young at heart, I'll grant you that, but they're not so keen on climbing up a hill like this!'

The little group looked down on the landscape below them. They could see a train winding its way through the valley and the village where the centre was situated.

Guillaume was hesitant to say any more but Valérie broke the silence. 'It seems to me that we're not attracting the younger generation to our church. Young professionals like us, for example. I think that we need to be thinking this through as a fellowship.'

They could see that the pastor was feeling a bit vulnerable at this point. He couldn't deny what they were saying, but nothing in his seminary training had prepared him for this. How do you even start to go about consulting a church on such questions? He felt that most of the members, even the leadership team, probably thought that it was his job to lead the congregation. In any case, he was very aware that he was paid by them to do it!

Guillaume realized that this was the moment he was waiting for. 'Maybe we could set up something like we did at work when we wanted to get everyone on board as we looked at the future development of our company,' he suggested. 'We organized a learning community. I'll tell you about it as we go back down to the retreat centre.'

He saw the look of approval in Valérie's eyes as they all stood up and started back down the trail with Guillaume walking next to the pastor.

A village in central Romania

As his friend, Gheorghe, had recommended, Stefan signed up to join a year-round mentoring group organized by the European Leadership Forum. He chose the one on church revitalisation, which Gheorghe had mentioned.

At the first webinar, he met the rest of the group. What a range of countries the pastors came from – Hungary, Scotland, Spain, Slovakia, Poland and

Sweden – but they were all facing the same questions about reinvigorating their church life, each in their own context.

The very first session was called 'An honest look at the situation in your church'. This was the initial step of the journey on which they were embarking. One of the mentors started by quoting Socrates who said, 'An unexamined life is not worth living.' The mentor added, 'An unexamined church is not worth serving.'

They all agreed that the very first stage of the revitalisation process had to be an assessment of the current situation in the church, but what was the best way to do this? Some of the participants thought that an anonymous questionnaire completed by church members would be a good approach. Another pastor suggested setting up a learning community, but Stefan couldn't grasp the concept. In his rural Romanian context, he thought, the best thing would be to try to talk to people in the church – quite informally at first – and he was encouraged that a pastor from central Europe agreed with him.

The discussion turned to the big issue that many leaders won't admit openly: fear of change. One of the mentors stressed that it is impossible to revitalise a church on your own. The pastor needs to work with a team, however small, so that there can be mutual support when opposition rears its head and mutual stimulation to think in new ways about church life. In short, fears can be relieved by mentoring from the outside and from backing within the church.

After the webinar, Stefan went to the kitchen where Ana was cooking the evening meal. 'I've just had a fantastic couple of hours of sharing with a group of pastors I didn't even know before our video meeting,' he enthused. He explained about the need for a team, but he was puzzled about who he could approach in the church. 'Ana, you're so good at observing people and seeing what makes them tick. Can you think of anyone in the church I could approach about the need for change?'

Ana thought for a moment and mentioned two men and a woman. Then she added, 'But I want you to know that I'm with you on this too, my love. It won't be easy. People are struggling to provide for their families and raise their children. They don't necessarily want to get involved in more activities.' Stefan nodded and Ana continued, 'And I don't want you to suffer from burnout. I've been reading a book about this. It explained that burnout doesn't come from overwork but from trying to meet different expectations within the congregation. Pastors haven't been trained to deal with this. Before we got married,

I was a social worker. That could be useful. Couldn't I be part of your revitalisation team, as you call it?'

Stefan asked Ana to put down the saucepan she was holding so that he could give her a big hug. 'I thank the Lord every day for giving you to me as my wife. I love you!'

'Well, we're going to need a lot of tender love and care for others as we seek to help our struggling church,' Ana concluded.

5
Getting started with change

I am sitting in my study today. From my window (on the sixteenth floor of our block of flats), I have a great view across Paris. I can see the Eiffel Tower to my right and also the dome of Les Invalides (which was built by Louis XIV as a hospital for his wounded soldiers and now houses Napoleon's tomb). I am the pastor of a church in Paris so I know where I am as writer of these pages. But who are you?

If you are the pastor or a member of the leadership team of a local church, then you can begin the process of revitalisation. If you are a church member, then you will have to convince the leadership to look at this issue – maybe by lending them this book! In any case, the process will be a long haul. It will sometimes be tough. But it will only happen if the church leadership is committed to it.

In his book *Comeback Churches*,[1] Ed Stetzer presents the findings of his research on revitalisation, recounting how '300 churches turned around' and sharing the main factors that led to change. Some of the statistics and approaches reflect his American context. The average size of attendance at the churches in the research was 266 and one church suggested that one way to renew your church was to employ two advertising experts on your staff. This is far beyond where we are in Europe but the book is still helpful if you bear in mind the cultural differences, just as this book might be useful for American churches, particularly if they are smaller or in culturally 'post-Christian' areas.

One finding applies to every continent of the world. As Stetzer puts it, 'Everything rises and falls on leadership.'[2] Based on his research, he writes, 'Leadership was rated as the number one factor by the churches

---

1 Ed Stetzer, *Comeback Churches: How 300 Churches Turned Around and Yours Can Too* (Nashville, TN: B & H, 2007).
2 Stetzer, *Comeback Churches*, p. 34.

that experienced revitalisation. Leadership and vision are the major keys to any type of turnaround in churches.'[3] But unfortunately, leadership can also be the major obstacle to revitalisation. Stetzer quotes the Barna Group: 'In this time of unprecedented opportunity and plentiful resources, the church is losing influence. The primary reason is the lack of leadership. Nothing is more important than leadership.'[4]

Some very interesting statistics come out of Stetzer's research on the role of leadership in revitalisation. These could have some relevance to our thinking, as long as we remember that these are just tendencies and not universal truths:

- '75% of comeback church pastors are over 40 years of age.'[5]
- 'They are more educated than the average pastor: 79% are graduates, in fact 51% have more than a first degree.'[6]
- '40% of comeback churches changed without changing their senior pastor.'[7]

In my experience, the biggest factor in getting leaders and church members committed to bringing about change is that they come to the realization that the pain of staying the same will be greater than the pain of change. To use a metaphor from air travel, they must put their own oxygen mask on before they try to help others.

Before starting, it would be useful to take an overview of where we are going, a road map of the revitalisation process that we will be following.

Personally, I have found it useful to become acquainted with change management and to understand the current thinking on this subject. I have been impressed to see how similar most models of change management are. Whether they are applied to a company, an NGO or a church, the same principles apply. The reason for this is obvious: we are dealing with human beings in all their complexity and even redeemed humans, saved by grace, are still working on their sanctification. As a Christian leader, I know that we will never achieve perfection on this earth.

---

3 Stetzer, *Comeback Churches*, p. 34.
4 Stetzer, *Comeback Churches*, p. 14.
5 Stetzer, *Comeback Churches*, p. 187.
6 Stetzer, *Comeback Churches*, p. 188.
7 Stetzer, *Comeback Churches*, pp. 177–178.

The classic eight steps involved in change management are:

1 create a sense of urgency
2 assemble a team to lead the process
3 develop the vision and strategy for change
4 communicate so that people understand and adhere to the vision
5 involve as many people as possible
6 produce short-term gains
7 persevere
8 create a new culture

Before we look at the practicalities of revitalisation in a local church situation, I would like to unpack these steps so that we can see where we are going.

Create a sense of urgency

Without a feeling that something has to change, church revitalisation is not possible. People satisfied with the status quo will not want to move out of their comfort zone.

Assemble a team to lead the process

No single individual can reconnect a church.

Develop the vision and strategy for change

The revitalisation team will look at the condition of the church and its values carefully, whether or not these values are stated formally. They will investigate the different options in their particular context in order to envisage working towards the vision of a healthy church as gathered and scattered. This is a mental picture of what the church will look like when it reaches the destination of the revitalisation journey but, before the process is set in motion, the team must try to start with an accurate picture of where the church is now.

Communicate so that people understand and adhere to the vision

The starting point is to explain (in positive terms) the reasons for the changes. The ideal outcome is that people desire to enter into the vision when they understand the reason for the innovations. However, it is part of human nature to resist change and the revitalisation team must know how to deal with this. Remember that communication is not a one-off event but needs to be ongoing.

Involve as many people as possible

The best way forward is to encourage others to become involved, organizing training where necessary and giving them the power to act.

Produce short-term gains

This is an aspect of change that is often forgotten. The team can set some achievable goals by finding things that can be changed relatively easily. As a friend says, pick the lowest hanging fruit and then celebrate. This is important for younger generations.

Persevere

It is very easy to wander back to old ways, to the culture of doing things in the way that you are used to as a default position. It is tempting to take the foot off the pedal because of the effort it takes to keep going. The revitalisation team should therefore remain in place for some time to track progress and to adjust (and hopefully improve) their plans.

Create a new culture

The aim is to create a culture of continuous improvement. As the saying goes, 'Change is here to stay!' This new culture calls for good leadership and a certain degree of strategic planning.

At the end of this chapter, you will find a flow chart of the process of revitalisation. Personally, I find it helpful to have the whole procedure in this visual form in order to see the different stages more clearly. You may find it useful to make a copy of the chart and keep it next to you while reading this book in order to follow the process more easily.

The first phase

To come back to the main thrust of this chapter, how do we start?

The necessary precondition for revitalisation is to acknowledge that there is a problem. If you are reading this book, it is probably because you already feel some discontent. You do not feel that you are growing as a Christian. You feel that your church is in too much of a bubble – a place of escape from day-to-day life rather than a community preparing and strengthening you to live for Christ in all you do. You feel that your church is disconnected from non-believers. You are looking for alternative ways of worshipping God. So, let's get going!

Create a sense of urgency

This needs a lot of grace in the ways that things are said so that it does not sound as though you are criticizing and complaining. There are several verses in the New Testament that warn us not to complain: 'These people are grumblers and faultfinders' (Jude 1:16); 'Do everything without grumbling or arguing' (Philippians 2:14). We should be encouragers of each other and build each other up (see 1 Thessalonians 5:11), but this can include what I call 'holy dissatisfaction'. We can ask questions such as:

- 'How can we do better?' (not 'What are we doing wrong?')
- 'How can we be holier?'
- 'How can we better love each other and those around us?'
- 'How can we do that in today's society?'

As you do this, you will find like-minded people who have a nagging feeling that something is not right and who see the need for change. This might come from a realization that the numbers of people attending the church are dropping or from any of the other signs mentioned in chapter 2. Very often, it comes from a recognition that the church and today's culture are disconnected from each other. In other words, people are not truly hearing the gospel message, partly because it is hidden by traditions and practices from another age. But the real urgency comes from the need for the church to be healthy, to better love God and to better love others as opposed to an unhealthy urgency that is simply concerned with promoting the local church as an institution for its own sake or for our personal benefit.

Assemble a team to lead the process

This is an important step to take. Even before the whole church is on board, it will be necessary to assemble a team to lead the revitalisation process. Hopefully, this will be led by the pastor and include several people from the leadership team. By leadership, I mean to include the various ways in which a local church is organized according to denominational background and the legislation regarding churches in each country. A leadership team may be a pastoral team (elders or bishops, to use the New Testament vocabulary), a church board (or council) or a mixture of both. Paul's image of the body in 1 Corinthians 12, for example, shows how the church needs a variety of gifts to function well. The list of gifts does not appear to be exhaustive, so what gifts might be necessary within a revitalisation team?

There should be a visionary in the team, and also someone who is a completer or finisher who will make sure that the project reaches its goal because not every visionary can deal with multiple practical issues. The revitalisation team should also include influencers, whether they have been appointed or elected to formal roles of responsibility in the church or not. There are different types of influencers: likable people who build relationships easily and bring people together; technically minded people who can easily analyse facts and figures; communicators who can present these findings to a group; and so on. These people are sometimes called 'change champions'. They are open to new ideas, they are good at networking and they are willing to take risks.

Research has shown how important it is to include different types of people in a team. Dr Meredith Belbin states that nine clusters of behaviour are needed on a team. Fortunately, that does not mean that you must have a team of nine people. Most people can take on two or three of these roles.[8]

In an ideal situation, the team will be approved by a meeting of the church members and therefore empowered to bring about change, but it would also suffice if the leadership team takes the lead because they have already been recognized by the members and they can co-opt other members into hearing new perspectives on the process. However, transparency in the choice of the team members and regular communication accessible to everyone are essential in order to avoid church members saying, '*They* have done this or that,' rather than, '*We* are doing it.'

Change requires both authority and trust, so the team needs to work within the structures and decision-making processes of the church. Change also needs to happen at a speed that does not outrun the trust that people have in their leaders or the revitalisation team.

---

8 You can learn more at "The Nine Belbin Team Roles," www.belbin.com/about/belbin-team-roles.

At the outset, the main qualifications for this team are very simple:

- They must see the need for revitalisation (though they may have no idea how to go about it in the beginning).
- They must be prayerful and spiritually mature. Their hunger for God and his glory must be their motivation in order to avoid falling into a purely technical mindset about change.
- They must be prepared to work towards solutions even though there may be a high cost in terms of time and effort, especially as far as the sensibilities and resistance to change of church members are concerned.
- Where appropriate, they should be open to seeking coaching from outside the church. This may be from their denomination, from attending a seminar or by being accompanied by a facilitator (either by in-person visits or online).
- They should become acquainted with the principles of change management.
- They will focus on working first and foremost towards being a healthy church: a fellowship of believers, redeemed through the gospel, who are learning to love God with all their heart, with all their soul, with all their mind, with all their strength (Mark 12:30) and to love people (Mark 12:31) in their cultural context.

I know I keep repeating this, but it is important not to measure revitalisation by numbers alone.

Understanding change management

An important component of biblical teaching concerns the need for wisdom. Whole books of the Old Testament (such as Proverbs and Ecclesiastes) are known as wisdom literature and the book of James, which promotes a similar approach to life, has an amazing promise: 'If any of you lacks wisdom, you should ask God, who gives generously to all without finding fault, and it will be given to you' (James 1:5).

In every human culture, we find proverbs and stories built up over the centuries to help people consider what it looks like to live life in a wise way. In our continually changing Western society, what is known as change management is an attempt to deal with change wisely. As long as we bear in mind that spiritual renewal is not purely a matter of human dynamics, we can draw on this wisdom. It is a matter of God working in us, though that does not negate the human side of change.

An easy-to-read book on change management is *Our Iceberg Is Melting* by John Kotter and Holger Rathgeber.[9] I highly recommend it. It is the story of a penguin who discovers that the iceberg where he lives is in danger of melting, but how can he persuade the whole colony to find a safer place to live? The story takes us through the whole process of change until the penguins finally decide to – well, you'll have to read the book to find out how it all ends. I find this book to be a real encouragement and a handy road map as you set out on the journey of revitalisation. It is also a useful book to lend to church members in the hope that they will see the humorous side of change and hopefully take their objections and resistance to change a little less seriously.

Revitalisation: bringing about change in order to work towards being a healthy church

Getting started
Create a sense of urgency
Assemble a team to lead the process (where appropriate, seek coaching from outside the church)
Understand change management

↓

Developing an appropriate strategy for change based on the vision of a healthy church
Assess the state of the church together
Own the realistic, exciting biblical vision of a healthy church and work towards a strategy for change

↓   ↓   ↓

---

9 John Kotter and Holger Rathgeber, *Our Iceberg Is Melting: Changing and Succeeding Under Any Conditions* (Penguin Random House, 2016).

Getting started with change

Spiritual	Social	Societal
Improving the spiritual health of the church	Improving relationships within the church and with non-believers	Improving the contextualization of the church
The centrality of the gospel Worshipping God with a sense of wonder, reverence and creativity in a way that is also accessible to non-Christians Earnest prayer	Face-to-face relationships Mutual support and encouragement Prayer for each other Hospitality	Living in today's culture and responding to the needs in the community around the church
Discipleship in order to build a relationship with God Learning to trust and obey God 24/7 Increasing knowledge of Scripture by teaching and dialogue (adults learn by talking to each other)	Discipleship in order to live well as the scattered church Sent by Jesus into the world to build relationships, to do good and to share the gospel in four relational networks: family, work or education, community and leisure time or friends	Discipleship in order to have a relevant witness Understanding today's society and helping Christians to speak into the issues

↓

Starting the movement
Communicate so that people understand and adhere to the vision and the strategy for change
Involve as many people as possible
Produce short-term gains
Persevere

↓

Working towards lasting change
Structural
Improving the quality of leadership within the church
Encourage the concept of a 'hybrid church' that is both gathered and scattered Put good leadership and decision-making systems into place
Strategic
Creating a new culture of ongoing change
Avoid falling back into routine by: • continually evaluating whether members are being helped to grow spiritually and to reach out with the gospel • discerning what can be done intentionally and what can simply be committed to God in prayer

Figure 3 **The revitalisation flow chart**

A small town near Manchester, UK

The four couples got together for a meal the following Friday evening. They were a little bit ill at ease at first because they didn't know each other very well. Of course they greeted each other at church every Sunday and exchanged banal words about the service and the weather, but there was an 'agenda' this evening and no one was sure how much they should open up to each other.

As usual, Carol was superb. She had a real talent for making people feel at ease. Jane had already been in Martin and Carol's home but it was the first time for Margaret Chapman and Sue Wyatt. They chatted in the kitchen, admiring the design and the amount of workspace. Meanwhile, the men talked about football, a pretty safe subject as long as you supported the same team. Unlike Tom and Martin, Trevor Chapman and Roger Wyatt never went to any of the local team's matches but they were proud of their town and followed the team's progress on the internet. At seven o'clock, the pizzas arrived and they spent the next thirty minutes discussing the Wyatts' experience of pizza in Italy and swapping stories about their recent holidays.

Tea and coffee were served and Martin cleared his throat and thanked everyone for agreeing to meet in their home to talk about the church. He thanked Trevor for his commitment as an elder and made it clear that the aim of the evening was not to criticize the leadership of the church but to share ideas about how it could be – Martin hesitated as he looked for a neutral word – *developed* in today's world.

'As far as I can see,' Martin continued, 'we need to reconnect the church to where people are today. The words we use and the subjects we talk about don't resonate with people in our town. We seem irrelevant. We don't link what we believe to the issues people are talking about.' He suddenly realized that he was doing all the talking and finished a bit flatly, 'What do the rest of you think?'

There were a few moments of silence and Martin wondered if some of the group were embarrassed by what he had said.

Then Trevor spoke up. 'I'd just like to say that we have brought up this subject in our elders' meetings, but we simply didn't know how to take it any further. You don't need to worry that you'll be seen as a sort of protest movement! The important thing is to work together, but I'm afraid I don't know where we should begin.'

Trevor's wife Margaret was often seen as a rather self-effacing woman, so everyone was startled when she piped up, 'Why don't we just ask all the church members for their ideas?'

Carol, always the realist, asked whether that could be done in a church where people didn't know each other very well, but her husband suggested that Roger Wyatt might have some ideas as a management consultant. Everyone turned towards Roger to hear what he might have to say.

'One thing we often do is ask people to fill in an anonymous questionnaire,' Roger suggested.

'Do you think people would do that?' asked Jane.

'We're always being asked to do that today,' Tom jumped in. 'People are used to it. Whenever I travel somewhere or buy something online, I always get a message asking me to rate my experience!'

Roger went on, 'In our case, that would help us to get to know the church members and find out how they're involved in the local community. And we could ask them, for example, what two changes they would like to see in the church. I think it's feasible.'

Trevor agreed to bring it up at the next elders' meeting and said that he would invite Roger along to explain it all in more detail.

The decision was made. Things were beginning to move, everyone was more relaxed and the weekend lay ahead. What more could they ask for?

A city in the west of France

Madame Christine Leclerc was puzzled. Two weeks before, at the end of the morning service, pastor Denis had announced that the leadership team had decided to organize a 'learning community' to talk about the development of the church. She had no idea what a learning community was and the idea that a church needed development had never crossed her mind. She was seventy years old, a widow for several years since her husband had died unexpectedly from a heart attack at work. She and her husband had become Christians through the witness of a neighbour and she had been a faithful member of the church ever since. She enjoyed the services. She thought that pastor Denis was a good preacher and she helped to prepare the monthly fellowship meals. She had made several good friends among the ladies in the church. But the idea of 'developing' a church was a mystery to her. In fact, she had hardly ever visited another church except for the annual interchurch prayer meeting at the beginning of January as part of the Evangelical Alliance Week of Prayer. She had very little idea of the diversity among evangelical churches and couldn't imagine a church being different from the one she attended week after week.

But here she was one Saturday afternoon, sitting around a table with six other people. There were another eight or nine similar tables and most of the adults in the church were there. She wondered where all the families had found babysitters – when her children were young it had been hard to find someone to watch them. She was sitting next to Valérie, which reassured her. Christine didn't know her very well but had always found her to be very friendly.

Pastor Denis stood up and introduced another man by the name of Marc. He was one of the leaders of their denomination who had come over from Paris for the weekend. Marc started by quoting some Latin: *ecclesia semper reformanda*, meaning 'the church must always be reforming'.

Christine felt at a bit of a loss but Valérie smiled and whispered to her, 'I don't know any Latin either.'

Fortunately, after the baffling start, Marc got going and showed a diagram of a healthy church. Christine felt relieved that she could easily relate to that graphic. Then Marc explained that they were going to think together about three things that were important in any church: how to improve the quality of their relationships, especially with people outside the church; how to be more relevant in communicating the message of the gospel; and how to grow in their relationship with God. He spent the next fifteen minutes showing how Jesus and the early Christians invested their time in building relationships with each other and their circle of friends and acquaintances.

Then came the biggest surprise for Christine. Pastor Denis told the whole group that they were going to discuss the subject around their tables and write their responses on the flip charts set up beside them.

'The two questions we are going to discuss are quite simple,' added Denis. 'What did you hear? And what does that mean for us in our church?'

Timothée, a young father of two children, was chosen to write down the comments for the group that Christine was part of. At first she felt rather shy and let the others talk, but Timothée asked her directly how she found ways to build significant relationships with non-Christians and Christine told him that she belonged to a knitting group that met in a social centre near her home. Timothée wrote it on the board. Then Valérie got Timothée to write down that the church should make it easier for younger people such as Guillaume and herself to meet with their friends on Saturday nights. At first Christine couldn't understand – she was always in bed by ten o'clock – but Valérie patiently explained that the issue was the lifestyle of their friends and Christine began to see the problem.

Half an hour later, every group shared what they had discussed. Christine blushed when everyone clapped for her idea of the knitting group, but deep down she was proud that she had contributed to the learning community.

A village in central Romania

Stefan and Ana decided to go together to meet the people they had identified as a possible revitalisation team. They had agreed on a method that was unusual for them: meeting the people in their everyday situations.

The next morning, they took their car to the local garage. It was owned by Marius, a member of the church council. The car needed a new tyre so they had a good excuse for their visit, but it also gave them the chance to have a chat. As they had half expected, Marius invited them to stay while his mechanic did the work.

'Come into my office, pastor,' he said. 'It's nice to see you together outside of the church. Would you like a coffee? There's a fresh pot here.'

'Your garage seems to be thriving,' remarked Stefan, 'judging by the number of cars waiting to be repaired.'

'Well, I haven't got much competition in the village,' laughed Marius. 'And most people can't afford to buy a new car so they need me to keep their old ones on the road.'

'You must see half the village in the course of the year. And I know that your work is highly regarded,' added Ana. 'Do they know that you're a Christian and that's why your prices are so fair?'

Marius pondered the question. 'I'm not sure. Although it would be great if that was the case. How could I communicate that to my customers?'

Stefan jumped at the opportunity. 'That's why I'd like to form a team in the church to think about how we can live as Christians – and show it – all through the week.'

A few minutes later, Stefan and Ana, pleased that Marius had accepted their offer to join the new group, made their way to the home of a young mother, Sofia. She had grown up in Bucharest and had moved to the village when she got married. The pastoral couple had noticed that she was less wary of 'the world' than most of the church members who feared the bad influence that society had on people's morals. She was always the first to try to befriend the other mothers at the school gate. Her husband, Florin, followed her example and had joined the village football team where he was one of the leading goalscorers. Ana explained their plans and, the next day,

Sofia phoned them to say that she and her husband were on board and would like to be part of the team.

Two days later, Stefan and Ana prayed that God would show them which of the elders of the church they could contact. This would be a very strategic decision. How would they know who best to approach?

That evening, after the church Bible study when the other participants had left, Grigore, one of the elders, stayed to talk to Stefan. Grigore was what people called a chatterbox, but he was quite a learned man and was never boring.

'That was a great chapter we did tonight, Stefan. Romans 15. Wow! Paul talks of the gospel going from Jerusalem to Illyricum – that's not so far from us in fact – and then to Rome and Spain. He wanted everyone to hear the gospel. But what about us here in this village? I think that our church has too much of a "siege mentality". We should get out into the village community more. What do you think?'

Stefan was speechless. He showed Grigore a diagram that he had down-loaded from the ELF mentoring group, showing what a healthy church should look like, giving equal weight to the gathered church and the scattered church.

Grigore was enchanted. He agreed to join the revitalisation group. 'We must start thinking about people, not programmes,' he threw out.

'Not a bad slogan,' Stefan thought. He was sure that he would use it before the year was out.

Stefan reflected that God had answered their prayer about which elder to contact. 'God is "able to do immeasurably more than all we ask or imagine",' he thought, 'just as Paul wrote to the Ephesians.'[10]

---

10 Ephesians 3:20.

6

The process: developing
a strategy for change

In the flow chart showing the stages of the revitalisation process, the second stage is called 'developing an appropriate strategy for change based on the vision of a healthy church'. There are two aspects to this:

1 assessing the state of the church together
2 owning the realistic, exciting biblical vision of a healthy church
   and working towards a strategy for change

In fact, these two aspects go together because they both involve seeing or vision. There are two ways to define vision: sight (i.e., the act or faculty of seeing) and imaginative insight or foresight. I believe that these two meanings are illustrated by the prophets of the Old Testament. According to 1 Samuel, 'Formerly in Israel, if someone went to inquire of God, they would say, "Come, let us go to the seer," because the prophet of today used to be called a seer' (1 Samuel 9:9). The prophets were able to see. They first saw the present reality of the people of Israel (a great deal of prophetic proclamation describes the sinful behaviour of God's people) and then they saw the projected outcome depending on whether the people repented of their sins or not.

In the same way, though on a different level, the revitalisation team will seek an accurate picture of the present reality. In other words, they will be lucid, clear-sighted and realistic about their church and its context (i.e., the surrounding society). They will have a vision of what a healthy church is and endeavour to identify the means and the strategy which will take them there.

In this chapter, we will look at ways of assessing the state of the church and owning the vision. Then, in the following chapters, we will look at specific ways of developing an appropriate strategy for the spiritual, social and societal aspects of revitalisation.

Assessing the state of the church together

There are four ways to get a picture of what I call *the present reality*. You should think about which ones would be most appropriate in your context.

Option 1: conduct a questionnaire or survey for the church leaders

The first stage is for the revitalisation team to look at the church and to think through the issues with the church leaders. The following questions are a useful guideline, which will also help the team to evaluate the degree of urgency by situating the church on the membership curve: plateau, decline or death (see the diagram in chapter 1). To put it differently, is the church stable but needing change, in crisis or in danger of extinction?

Survey for church leaders

On church

1 What is the average attendance at your main Sunday meeting?
   (a) Has this changed over the past five years?
   (b) Are the members of the church satisfied with this number?
2 Has the average age of the adult attendance changed over the past five years?
   (a) How would you describe the age range across the members of your church?
   (b) Are there any gaps?
3 Do the members know each other well?
   (a) Have people from outside the church been converted through the ministry of the church in the past five years?
   (b) Are the majority of members actively involved in the life and ministry of the church?

On the church leadership

4 How many people are involved in the leadership of the church
   (a) in a pastoral role?
   (b) in a diaconal role?

5 Is there a strong sense of unity among the leaders?
   (a) Do the leaders meet regularly to pray together?
   (b) What sort of subjects do you as a leader have on your heart?
6 Do you as a leader feel the need for more training in order to better serve the church?
7 Do you as a leader need help as you think through the ways that churches can build up Christians and reach out to non-Christians in today's society?
8 Does the leadership encourage the church to pray for the gospel to change lives both within the church and through evangelism?

On vision

9 Does the leadership team have a clear vision for the church? Can you write this vision down in a few short sentences?
10 If there is a vision, do the members of the church know it and adhere to it?
11 Does the leadership regularly review the effectiveness of the church's ministries in relation to the vision?
12 What do you wish that the church would look like in five years' time, to the glory of God?

On the surrounding area

13 In what ways has your local area changed over the past ten years?
14 Does the socio-economic profile of your church correspond to that of your local area?
15 Does the church have any ministries designed to serve the people in your local area?
16 Are you aware of any needs in your local area that your church could meet?
17 Are the members of your church involved in activities outside the church?

On presence

18 Do the majority of your church members live in the area where the church meets?
19 What reputation does your church have in your local area?
20 Is your church service conducted in such a way that a non-Christian from your area would be able to understand what was being said if they came to church?
21 Would a non-Christian from your area find your church building attractive, comfortable and welcoming?

Option 2: conduct a questionnaire or survey for the congregation

Of course the church leaders may not have all the answers. For some, it could be a painful exercise. Others may never have considered some of these issues. In his book *Comeback Churches*, Ed Stetzer draws a distinction between managers and leaders: 'Management is doing things right. Leadership is doing the right things.'[1] In other words, we have to move from maintenance to strategic thinking, from efficiency (keeping things going and avoiding failure) to effectiveness (being proactive and innovative).

To help leaders to understand the state of the church, it is imperative to gather feedback from the members. I spoke to one specialist in church revitalisation who asserted that church members are often aware of the need for revitalisation before their leaders.

This is a sample questionnaire that can enable leaders to gather useful information on the state of their church from the point of view of the congregation. It can be used to gather assessments from people who are officially church members and from members of the congregation who have not taken this step. In any case, you can adapt it to your situation if some of the questions are irrelevant or if they would be seen as too direct in the culture in which you work. This survey can also be followed up by a meeting (or series of meetings) where interested members of the congregation can express their point of view and think the issues through.

Survey for congregation members: what future for our church?

Facing the future can be a very sensitive matter and can be deeply unsettling for any church. Many people have been faithful in their service to the Lord Jesus over a long period and may feel fearful about considering the future. However, this survey will prove to be a helpful exercise if you approach it in a prayerful, warm-hearted and open way.

Some questions in this survey are factual and others will help you to think about the life of the church. They are designed to help your leaders gather information about the church. Please ask the Lord in prayer to guide you as you answer each question.

---

1 Ed Stetzer, *Comeback Churches: How 300 Churches Turned Around and Yours Can Too* (Nashville, TN: B & H, 2007) p. 181.

About you
1 Are you male or female?
2 How old are you?
3 How long have you been a Christian?
4 How long have you been coming to this church?

You and your church
5 What do you think the main purpose of your church is?
6 Which aspects of church life have particularly encouraged you over the past five years?
7 Which aspects of church life have particularly discouraged you over the past five years?
8 How do you feel about the way that your church is led?
9 Other than what you already do, which gifts would you like the opportunity to exercise at church?
10 If you could change two things about your church, what would they be?
11 Which do you think is the most effective ministry in your church? In what way is it effective?
12 What would give you more confidence to invite friends and neighbours to services or meetings at your church?

You and the surrounding area
13 How far do you live from the building in which your church meets?
14 In what ways are you involved in the geographical area served by your church?
15 If your church had the people and finances, how could it better serve the surrounding area?
16 What impact would it have on the surrounding area if your church had to close?

You and the future
17 What would you most like to see happen in your church in the next five years?
18 What are you praying for in the life of your church right now?
19 Assuming that things continue in the same vein, how do you feel about the future of your church?
20 Is there anything else that you would like to tell us about your church?

These two questionnaires originally came from the UK church movement called the Fellowship of Independent Evangelical Churches (FIEC). I have adapted them for more general use based on my experience in France.[2]

I acknowledge that interpreting data from a survey is not always easy. The FIEC document also provides some guidance on the best way to examine the completed questionnaires. You may find the following extracts helpful.

Analysing the data

A core principle

Always have in mind the research question that you are trying to answer. In this case, it is defined as, 'What is the spiritual condition of this church and the mood of its congregation?' Analyse the data while keeping in mind what you are trying to find out and why the data was collected in the first place. Avoid 'data mining' to answer alternative questions and do not follow through on things just because you find them interesting.

Summarizing and interpreting the data

The analysis of the answers involves aiming to uncover and to understand the big picture in the church by using individual answers to describe what is going on. What are the big issues facing the church and the church members?

This type of analysis is hard because you are not dealing with hard facts and percentages. In fact, you should avoid quoting any percentages because it is likely that the sample size (i.e., the number of people who took the survey) is so small that the figures may be misleading.

Instead, you are looking to recognize overarching themes in the data. Are there any common themes coming across from different parts of the surveys? Identify salient themes, recurring ideas or language, and patterns of opinion that link together. You are looking for an overall 'feel'. This is the most challenging phase of the analysis.

---

2 Used and adapted by permission. For more information see www.fiec.org.uk. If you wish to use these surveys, you can find them in printable form at www.revitalisation.fr/en/tools. I recommend this bilingual (English and French) revitalisation site for a range of useful documents and videos.

In particular, you should look for:

- words or phrases that are used frequently
- patterns, themes and trends
- gaps (for example, no twenty- to thirty-year-olds in the church)
- evidence of the way that the church may have changed in the past few years
- the overall tone of the responses – are they short or lengthy? Positive or negative?
- anything unexpected where our preconceptions are challenged or where we hear things that we were not expecting to hear

You should not put too much emphasis on the views of any particular individual as they may not be representative of the whole. However, consider the possibility that they may be the first one who was prepared to admit some hard truths or the only one who has particular spiritual insight. It is often too easy to discard 'outliers' as they do not fit into the patterns and themes of the data, but it is just as important to examine these things carefully and to consider the possible explanations for these different views.

You should also acknowledge the factors that might have influenced participant responses: the time of day, the time of year, the weather, where the questionnaires were completed, whether the participant is likely to have discussed their answers with anyone else in the church or any particular issue in the church at that time.

The process of 'content analysis' is lengthy and may require you to go over and over the questionnaires in order to ensure that you have done a thorough job of analysis.

Option 3: interview people

Interviews are a way to gather qualitative evaluation from key people. They also enable you to hear feedback from non-members and from non-Christians without them being influenced by what others are saying or by how others may react when they hear what is said. This approach is particularly appropriate in more oral cultures where the idea of filling out evaluation forms is not widespread, or in church contexts that discourage public discussion of church affairs since this sort of deliberation is restricted to congregational or denominational leadership – in other words, where the expectations of church members do not include questionnaires.

Some pastors might wonder, 'Why do I need to interview people? I'm talking to people all the time about the problems they have with my church!' but structured interviews might well break new ground and they do not have to be conducted by the pastor him- or herself.

Option 4: the church meeting

I think that the best way to organize a church meeting is to use the 'learning community' approach. This type of meeting is sometimes called 'results-based conversation', 'results-driven conversation' or 'outcome-focused conversation'.

This structured approach has two advantages over a meeting that is not directed. First, it gives the revitalisation team (or the pastor and leaders) the opportunity to communicate facts and ideas about the need for revitalisation. They must be the ones who take the initiative for change. After all, they usually have more knowledge of the wider evangelical world than most members and often have a greater realization of the spiritual implications of today's culture. They need to keep the goals of the learning community in mind: to communicate the vision and to conduct conversations that lead to outcomes expressed in sentences including words such as 'in order to'.

Second, the church members are involved in discussing how to take that presentation into account and how to move on together. As a result, the church as a whole accepts the changes more positively and may suggest good ways of reaching the goal.

So what would that look like in practice? The ideal scenario is to have a day-long meeting, or at least a whole afternoon. Each session needs a speaker and an organizer and should open and close with a time of prayer.

The speaker begins the meeting by explaining the vision using the diagram of a healthy church in chapter 4. The meeting is then divided into three sessions, each with the same format, looking at the three areas of church life identified on the revitalisation flow chart (which can be found at the end of chapter 5). The best order to deal with these objectives is:

1 improving relationships within the church and with non-Christians
2 improving the contextualization of the church
3 improving the spiritual health of the church

The speaker should take fifteen minutes to develop the thoughts on these three aspects of revitalisation. After this short talk, the participants are divided into groups of four, five or six (no more) around tables. They discuss two questions together:

- What did I hear?
- What could that mean for our church? You can also use a similar wording such as 'what does this entail, indicate, call for?'

Each table should have a big sheet of paper on which the participants write down their main ideas. This should take twenty-five minutes.

Afterwards, the participants come back together into the big group and the papers from each table are displayed at the front of the room. Each table quickly explains what they wrote (this should take between ten and fifteen minutes), then the organiser asks the whole group to identify the ideas that have been mentioned most frequently. These can be highlighted on the papers and this should take a further ten minutes.

It is important to keep things moving fairly quickly. The ideas on the sheets, in particular those which have been highlighted, are important to help the revitalisation team to draw up an action plan.

Owning the vision and developing a strategy for change

Before developing a strategy for change, it is essential that the revitalisation team and then the church as a whole own the vision of a healthy church, which we looked at in chapter 4. The diagram is an excellent tool for communicating this in today's world where most people find it easier to process information that is presented in a visual format than in a document or a talk.

However, we must understand that this vision is not a detailed blueprint of the way forward. It is not like an architect's comprehensive and meticulous designs, including plumbing, all the electric circuits, and the heating and lighting systems. It is more like the artist's impression of the finished building. A vision is seeing the end from the beginning. The church members should be able to imagine it and to think it feasible and desirable. It should touch the head and the heart. The vision will help church members to understand more clearly why specific changes are being proposed. Without the vision, it might seem to be change for change's sake.

One difficulty I often come across is that many people find it difficult to think outside the box. The only church that they have ever seen is the one that they are in and they cannot imagine that things can be different. This may even apply to the church leaders. This is another reason why I indicated in the flow chart that coaching from outside the church may be a good option.

Once this overall vision is clear, the revitalisation team can use the information gleaned through the assessment stage to start to build a strategy for change. When this strategy is advanced sufficiently, it should be presented to the church in order to gather feedback from the members and (hopefully) approval for the main points of the project.

The definitive action plan should answer the following questions based on the leadership team's and the congregation's vision of a healthy church:

- What must we do to move towards our vision of a healthy church?
- When must we do these things?
- What specific tasks are involved?
- Who is responsible for each task?

The revitalisation team should draw up a calendar of the order in which the actions could be implemented. However, it would be wise not to communicate the whole action plan to the church at once but just the immediate steps that are being suggested for the following few months. You have to give it time. People need to get used to each new development and it would be a mistake to rush things.

No two churches will build a strategy for change in the same way and the action plan must be appropriate for your context. For too long, evangelical churches have suffered from a 'cut-copy-paste' syndrome where leaders look at a 'successful church' and attempt to do the same thing in their context. Let's be creative instead! Each church has its own set of values, either clearly stated or assumed and, as long as they do not stand in the way of revitalisation, these must be respected.

The strategy will be built up by focusing on three aspects: spiritual, social and societal. Ideally, they should all be worked on at the same time but it might be advisable in your action plan to put the emphasis on each of these aspects in turn. In that case, I would encourage you to start with the social dimension with a view to improving relationships within the church and with non-Christians. As Christians begin to interact with their non-Christian friends and neighbours, they will realize more keenly the cultural and spiritual gap between Christian faith and most people's perspectives on life. Hopefully, this will lead to a new eagerness to understand today's society (this is what I mean by the societal aspect) and to learn how to speak to their circle of family, friends and acquaintances in a relevant way. This will have an impact on the spiritual dimension of revitalisation as we walk with God in our context. In one sense, the spiritual side should be foremost but my experience has shown me that the way that we live as a church will depend on coming to terms with the culture in which we live. Remember that a healthy church is a place where Christians learn to love God and love people in their cultural context.

In the following chapters, we will look at these three aspects and think about what revitalisation will look like in practice as we begin to develop a strategy for change.

THE SOCIAL DIMENSION OF REVITALISATION

Love your neighbour as yourself.
Mark 12:31

A small town near Manchester, UK

Tom loved football and classical music. He could never understand why some people thought that this combination of pastimes was strange. His favourite composer was probably Johann Sebastian Bach. Attending a concert of the *St Matthew Passion* had been an emotional experience for him and, several times a year, he listened to a recording of Glenn Gould playing *The Art of the Fugue*. He always found it strangely moving when the unfinished fugue, 'Contrapunctus XIV', ended abruptly while the music was in full flow.

Tonight, Tom and Jane had tickets for a unique event in their town. A world-famous organist was performing a selection of Bach's works at the Anglican church. That was just too good to miss!

As they walked to the town centre, Tom explained enthusiastically to Jane why he loved Bach's music. 'It's so rational and yet so uplifting at the same time. Yes, it progresses logically, but if you press the stop button you're never quite sure where it's going next. And as a Christian, I fully understand this music in our fallen world. When it's melancholic, there's an underlying note of joy. And when it's joyful, Bach doesn't forget that darkness is never far away.'

Tom was already in a good mood because of the developments in their church. The leaders had set up a group to look into ways of transforming their church life. His friend Martin was one of the members of the group, as were Trevor (one of the elders) and Roger (the management consultant). The group had used a questionnaire to find out how the church members felt about things and the results were encouraging. There was a wider realization of the need for change than Tom had dared to hope for.

Now, as the organist started the recital, Tom was swept away by the *Toccata and Fugue*. For the next hour, he was totally entranced and his thoughts were led in myriad directions.

During the interval, he attempted to put his thoughts into words. Jane did her best to concentrate on what he was saying. In her relationship with Tom, she had taken to heart some words that she had read in Tolstoy's masterpiece *War and Peace*: '[Pierre] experienced now in telling it all to Natasha that rare happiness given to men by women when they listen to them … This rare happiness is given only by those real women, gifted with a faculty for picking out and assimilating all that is best in what a man shows.'[1]

---

1 Leo Tolstoy, *War and Peace,* trans. Constance Garnett (London: Heinemann, 1971) p. 1208.

Case study

'Listen, Jane,' Tom began. 'Don't you think that all of us live in three different but related stories? And Christians live in four!'

'I've never thought of that. What are they?' said Jane, encouraging him to go on.

'Well, first of all, every one of us has his or her individual life and we can make what we want of it – though hopefully that will include turning to Jesus for salvation.' Tom rushed on breathlessly, 'Next, for Christians, there's our church life and – as we're beginning to see – that doesn't need to be static. It can develop over the years.'

Jane smiled. Tom might not have said that a few weeks ago.

'Third,' Tom continued, 'there's the history of our nation that deeply affects the way that churches and Christians are seen by the media and the general public.'

'Do you mean the culture that we're in?' interjected Jane. 'It's like that missionary from India was telling us at church last week – the Hindu background there affects the way that people hear the gospel.'

'That's right, but we often don't realize the implications as far as our own culture is concerned. Then most importantly, there's God's plan unfolding over the centuries, which we can be part of.'

'You mean the whole Bible story?'

'Yes, that's it. Right from creation and the tragedy of sin entering the world – cutting humans off from God – then God's bridgehead with the patriarchs and the people of Israel until the time was ripe for Jesus to come into the world for our salvation. And today, we're living in the in-between time. The kingdom of God is already here but not in the fullness we'll one day know.'

'So it all fits together like a sort of tapestry, then?' One of Jane's hobbies was sewing.

'Exactly. It's a bit messy if you look at it from the back, which is all we can see, but God is working on the full picture. And that fits in with one of the main findings of the church survey we did. Most people wrote that they wanted to build deeper relationships in the church. But we all know that relationships can be a bit like a Bach fugue – unpredictable but fulfilling. And they can be messy, too, because none of us are perfect!'

'As I have loved you, so you must love one another. By this everyone will know that you are my disciples,' quoted Jane (John 13:34–35 were some of her favourite Bible verses).

Case study

They settled back into their seats for the second part of the concert, which included Bach's unfinished fugue. Tom always thought it was a bit like life: the tapestry was suddenly cut off by death. But as a Christian, he knew it was but the doorway to eternal life with God.

7

The social dimension of revitalisation: community

Aim: to improve relationships within the church

In the very first chapter of the Bible, we read about how human beings are the pinnacle of creation. We are the highest point of life on earth (and possibly in the universe). Our calling is to rule over the earth and we have managed to fulfil it. We occupy every part of the earth from the polar regions to the equator and have discovered so many resources that the lives of a high proportion of people on earth are easier than those of their ancestors.

From another perspective, we are just minuscule bipeds walking around on a very small planet which revolves around a rather insignificant star (which we call the sun) situated near the edge of one galaxy among millions of others. The dimensions of space are stupendous. At the speed of light, we could travel around the equator seven times in one second and we could reach the moon in two seconds. It would take four minutes to reach Mars and five hours to reach Pluto, at the edge of our solar system. But even at the speed of light, it would take over four years to reach the nearest star and 100,000 years to cross our galaxy (which we know as the Milky Way). If that was not mind-boggling enough, it would take 2 million years to reach the nearest galaxy to ours and cosmologists think that there are billions of galaxies.

That is the scale of our great God. Then, into all of this, comes the incredible thought process and decision of God: 'Let us make mankind in our image, in our likeness' (Genesis 1:26). And that is exactly what he did:

So God created mankind in his own image,
   in the image of God he created them;
     male and female he created them.
(Genesis 1:27)

Theologians have long tried to plumb the depths of the implications of this creation. First and foremost is the value of human life. 'Whoever sheds human blood, by humans shall their blood be shed; for in the image of God has God made mankind' (Genesis 9:6). James teaches us that, because we have been made in God's likeness, we should not curse our fellow human beings (see James 3:9).

Second, our humanity reflects some of the characteristics of God: the ability to think, to speak, to love, to be creative and to tell the difference between good and evil. This gives us the capacity to be stewards of God's creation here on earth.

Third, it means that we live in communities. Being created in God's image implies relationships because the Trinitarian God we worship exists eternally in the relationship between the Father, the Son and the Holy Spirit. The Father is unbegotten, the Son is eternally begotten of the Father, the Spirit is breathed out by the Father and the Son. Father, Son and Spirit love one another, coequal and coeternal. There is no hint of jealousy in the Godhead. 'God is love' (1 John 4:8, 16) and that is only possible because God is a triunity.

From the beginning, in Genesis, we see people linked together in families, tribes, and in villages and cities. We are interdependent. It started with procreation ('male and female he created them'). But, very rapidly, specialization crept in. For example, not everyone grew cereals and not everyone made shoes, so a complex system of exchange developed. In today's world, this is such an accepted fact that we can easily forget it. A few years ago, a designer wondered if he could make a toaster from scratch, but he discovered that even a simple model had four hundred parts made from one hundred different materials. Many of those materials (such as plastic) needed to be manufactured in a way that an individual could never reproduce, and the iron and nickel needed to be extracted from the ground and transformed into a usable form.

Above all, we need each other emotionally. Solitary confinement is one of the worst forms of punishment in a prison and, during the Covid-19 pandemic, being in lockdown was often extremely difficult for people living on their own, despite telephones and social media.

However, as soon as sin entered the world (see Genesis 3), the beauty of relationships was tarnished. Adam blamed Eve (see Genesis 3:12), the door was open for abuse (Genesis 3:16), shame entered the picture (see Genesis 3:7) and the man and the woman tried to hide (see Genesis 3:8). In the following chapter, we see the outworking of the rebellion against God with jealousy, violence, lying and self-centredness (see Genesis 4:9: 'Am I my brother's keeper?').

This is the world that we are in. Through God's common grace, the image of God remaining in us still spurs humans to acts of service and altruism. Very few people live as though the categories of good and evil do not exist, but they still need to be enforced. Why are we given a ticket for train travel? Why not just pay and use the train you paid for? Why does the railway need to employ ticket inspectors? One of my favourite films is *Tree of Life*, directed by Terrence Malick.[1] It illustrates perfectly the world that we are living in. A long sequence on the creation of the world is followed by the story of a 'normal' but dysfunctional family in America. There are moments of beauty when the parents contemplate the wonder of a newborn child, but we are also saddened by the regrets of the father who realizes that he has wasted his life trying to 'succeed' rather than spending time on building a more positive relationship with his sons.

All of this flows from Genesis 3, where the fundamental problem of humanity is made clear: the rebellious refusal to live God's way leads to separation from the Creator. Fortunately, there is a solution. The gospel brings us reconciliation with God, the forgiveness of our sins and the hope of everlasting life thanks to the sacrifice of Jesus who died in our place to bear the condemnation that we deserve. God can remain righteous and holy while still being a God of love. This is only possible at the cross.

God calls us to repent and believe. When we do this, two things happen. First, we are reconciled with God and we can start a relationship with him (John 17:3). Second, he starts to work in us to restore his tarnished image. This is a lifelong process known in theology as our 'sanctification'. If that word sounds off-putting, we can look at it another way: Jesus is the image of God (2 Corinthians 4:4) and we are called to be like him:

---

1 Terrence Malick, *Tree of Life*, 2011.

And we all, who with unveiled faces contemplate the Lord's glory, are being transformed into his image with ever-increasing glory, which comes from the Lord, who is the Spirit.
(2 Corinthians 3:18)

For those God foreknew he also predestined to be conformed to the image of his Son.
(Romans 8:29)

Reconciled with God, our aim is to be truly human as God restores his image in us. In this sense, Christians are to be the most human of all humans.

True spirituality is to be truly human and to build healthy relationships. It avoids legalism in which the Sabbath becomes more important than people (you can put any other man-made burden imposed on fellow believers in place of the Sabbath). It also avoids super-spirituality in which everyday pursuits are seen as less spiritual than religious activities, 'For everything God created is good, and nothing is to be rejected if it is received with thanksgiving' (1 Timothy 4:4).

However, in our daily lives, we can end up minimizing the importance of relationships and become very self-absorbed. Too often, we are in a bubble, rushing from one activity to another, one meeting to another, one task to another. Loving others takes time. Taking a real interest in others involves listening to them, encouraging them and doing good to them – three verbs we find in the New Testament.

So how does this apply to revitalisation? Let's look at the implications first within the church and then, in the next chapter, for our relationships with non-believers.

Relationships within the church

God has called us to be a people and to meet together as a people. It is not enough to simply 'go to church' and attend a service because that can become a legalistic duty. It is not enough just to sit next to someone and exchange a few words of greeting. It is not enough to simply be friendly because people are looking for true friends in Christ. I once heard someone say rather cynically, 'A Christian meeting is a time when you don't actually meet anyone.' That is certainly an exaggeration but, at the same time, there is a real danger of this happening. What a difference from the exhortations we read in Hebrews:

> Let us consider how we may spur one another on towards love and good deeds, not giving up meeting together, as some are in the habit of doing, but encouraging one another.
> (Hebrews 10:24–25)

The revitalisation team needs to think about how members of the church can begin to take responsibility for each other. Twice in this passage, we read the words 'one another'. In fact, this expression often occurs in the New Testament – generally (but not always) to translate the Greek word *allelous*. These moments fall into three categories (see opposite).

As I wrote above, the revitalisation team needs to think about how members of the church can begin to take responsibility for each other and how they can live out the 'one anothers'. What can you do to start moving in this direction and to nurture your church as a community?

First, teach what the church is according to the New Testament: a place where we can 'grow in the grace and knowledge of our Lord and Saviour Jesus Christ' (2 Peter 3:18) by worshipping him and becoming more like him. Use the Bible to show that this is a corporate, collective undertaking.

Second, use the times you meet together to help Christians get to know each other better. This can vary from church to church but, here in Paris, we have a church meal together every two weeks after both of our Sunday services (morning and evening). At lunchtime, everyone participates by bringing some food to share. In the evening, with a different congregation that comprises mainly younger people, we order pizzas from the pizza place just around the corner from our church building. We share stories, laugh together, sometimes bear each other's burdens (for example, illness or problems at work) and pray. We talk about jobs and sport and motorbikes. We talk about the Bible teaching that day. In short, we support each other in our walk with God in a way that will help us all through the week. This type of relationship can also be encouraged at Bible studies and prayer meetings. In summary, we need to be more human in the church and more spiritual in society.

Third, challenge people to build relationships with each other. This can be done through social media at the very least, but it is better to do so by speaking (for example, phoning each other) and best if it can be done

Category 1 Attitudes to one another

Love one another	John 13:34–35; 15:12; Romans 13:8; 1 John 4:12
Accept one another	Romans 15:7
Submit to one another	Ephesians 5:21
Bear with one another in love	Ephesians 4:2; Colossians 3:13
Forgive one another	Ephesians 4:32; Colossians 3:13
Spur one another on towards love and good deeds	Hebrews 10:24
Be kind and compassionate to one another	Ephesians 4:32
Live in harmony with one another	Romans 15:5
Have brotherly affection for one another	Romans 12:10
Be at peace with one another	Mark 9:50
Honour one another above yourselves	Romans 12:10; Philippians 2:3

Category 2 Words to one another

Speak to one another by singing	Ephesians 5:19
Encourage one another	1 Thessalonians 4:18; 5:11; Hebrews 10:25
Admonish one another	Colossians 3:16
Confess sins to one another	James 5:16
Pray for one another	James 5:16
Instruct one another	Romans 15:14

Category 3 Actions to one another

Care for one another	1 Corinthians 12:25–26
Be hospitable to one another	1 Peter 4:9
Serve one another in love	Galatians 5:13
Bear one another's burdens	Galatians 6:2

face to face. Video meetings are a good start, but being together in person is even better if time and geographical proximity allow it. I remember meeting a Christian woman in the Balkans who went to a coffee shop every day with a different sister in Christ for a time of spiritual encouragement. Individual initiatives are excellent but the church leaders can also offer some practical ways to do this by organizing prayer triplets, small 'growth groups' or by setting up weekly home groups so that people can share their lives through Bible study and prayer.

Fourth, encourage all sorts of hospitality. Several New Testament passages encourage us to be hospitable. Remember that the Greek word *koinonia* (meaning fellowship) includes sharing material possessions and can also be translated as 'solidarity'. It goes beyond just inviting some Christian friends for a meal, though that is a good place to start (as long as the aim is to enjoy each other's company and not simply to show off the quality of the cooking).

> Share with God's people who are in need. Practise hospitality.
> (Romans 12:13)

> Offer hospitality to one another without grumbling.
> (1 Peter 4:9)

Hospitality is a requirement for all Christians, including leaders. The ability to be hospitable is on the list of the criteria needed to be recognized as an elder (see 1 Timothy 3:2; Titus 1:8).

In one of the churches that I pastored, we had occasional 'hospitality Sundays' where some people offered to host a meal for a certain number of people and others put down their names as people who would like to be invited. In this way, people met other Christians they did not know very well and the life of the church family was strengthened. Our saucepans, kettles, knives and forks can be weapons in the spiritual battle to spread the gospel and to fight against the forces of darkness.

These are just a few practical suggestions. Be creative, think outside the box and ask church members for their ideas. What could work for you in your context?

A city in the west of France

No one in the church knew it but, since her teenage days, Valérie had dreamt of being an artist. She had realized soon enough that she wouldn't be able to make a career out of it, but she loved to paint in her spare time and Guillaume encouraged her to do this to help her to switch off from her high-pressure job. But it had come as a bit of a surprise to the group when, during the learning community, Valérie had suggested that the church might consider putting on an art exhibition.

This suggestion led to considerable debate at her table. Georges, a self-employed electrician, had never been to an art exhibition in his life and couldn't see what the connection with a church could possibly be. Maryse seemed to think that all modern art was a joke, exclaiming that her three-year-old niece could paint just like that. And Frédéric declared that the reason for art in a church ('Christian art' as he called it) was to illustrate stories from the Bible.

Valérie tried to convince them that there was something mysterious and allusive about art, something that went beyond the materials used – whether it was the catgut of violin strings, the paints used by the artist or the illusion created by pictures projected on a screen. 'Art produces emotions,' she argued. 'It makes us see and feel things that we wouldn't have experienced otherwise. In fact, I think that art can only be defined by the effects it produces on the audience – the listener, the viewer or the reader.'

These remarks only seemed to lead to more opposition.

Jacques was a very rational science teacher and was known for his deep commitment to propositional, scriptural teaching. 'I worry that art will lead us down the path to relativism,' he deplored. 'So many people today live by the principle that "whatever I feel deeply must be right."'

Valérie listened carefully and then brought out her strongest argument. 'I understand what you're all saying, but remember this: God has given us the gift of language. Art touches our emotions but we still think about it, analyse it and talk about it! An art exhibition is an invitation to start a dialogue with people or to help them see the relevance of the gospel, if you prefer. People are often hesitant to talk about themselves – their needs, their fears, their hopes – but they're more likely to open up while they're considering how art makes them feel. It could be a way of starting a genuine relationship with people.'

'So it's a form of evangelism then,' Georges blurted out. Everyone burst into laughter.

Frédéric couldn't help adding to the merriment. 'That's a good one, Georges. As an electrician, is that your *current* thinking?'

The atmosphere became completely relaxed and the group around the table agreed to write down the idea of an art exhibition on their flip chart.

A village in central Romania

When Stefan was appointed pastor of the church, he discovered that there was an event in the church's calendar that he could not skip. He had been doing some heart-searching about it for some time as he didn't feel at peace about it. He wasn't thinking of Christmas or Easter – of course they were also celebrated every year. It was the annual week of evangelism that was on his mind.

Every year during the first week of February, the whole church was mobilized for this special event. The church members put up posters and dropped flyers in every letterbox in the village. The younger people publicized it on social media. Every year a famous speaker (famous at least in the eyes of the church members) was invited to give a series of talks every evening for a week.

The budget for this event was considerable, what with the cost of printing and the honorarium paid to the preacher (which the church members called a thanksgiving gift).

But it wasn't the money that bothered Stefan. As he sat in his office at the back of the church building and tried to get his ideas straight, he realized that there were two reasons why he was more and more doubtful about the value of this approach to evangelism.

First, fewer and fewer people were turning up to these evenings. Maybe they knew what to expect and the novelty had worn off; maybe they didn't want to listen to a fiery preacher telling them that they were sinners; or maybe the latest series on the television just seemed more interesting.

And then there was a second reason for Stefan's unease. Why did evangelism only happen once a year? And why in that way?

Stefan picked up his phone and called Andrei, the pastor who had preceded him in the church. 'Hi Andrei. How are you? And your wife? I heard you just celebrated your eightieth birthday. Congratulations!' he started in a friendly tone. 'Hey, I've got a question I'd like to ask you. Were you the pastor who started the February evangelism week?'

Andrei chuckled. 'Good gracious, no. When I came to the church back in the soviet era, it was already a tradition. I was told, "That's the way we've always done it. God has always blessed that time. So we must faithfully continue in the same way." So I just went along with the tradition.'

'Thanks, Andrei. I hope you'll come and see us soon. We'd all like that.'

Stefan was puzzled. Why couldn't a church adapt to new contexts? After all, it wasn't the message of the gospel that was being changed, only the way that it was being communicated. Stefan was just old enough to have lived through several different periods of history as far as the Romanian churches were concerned. After severe persecution in the communist era, they had seen great blessings in the years following the fall of the Berlin Wall and many people had been converted. However, new ideas were coming in from Western Europe and Stefan wasn't sure whether he was preparing Christians to live in this new world. It wasn't just a question of evangelism but of being disciples of Jesus in this new world. Wasn't that why Christians were grouped together in churches, to encourage one other to follow Jesus faithfully all through the week? Wasn't that what it meant to be a healthy church?

He closed his office door, started to go home for lunch and looked in the church letterbox on the way. He found a couple of personal letters, a mission magazine and a flyer advertising the supermarket in the next town.

'Our special offers of the month,' it proclaimed. Stefan couldn't help thinking that the supermarket didn't just rely on one publicity event a year.

8

The social dimension of revitalisation: outreach

The aim: improving relationships with non-Christians

It is just as important that we build good relationships with those who are not (yet) Christians as it is with our brothers and sisters in the faith. 'If you greet only your own people, what are you doing more than others? Do not even pagans do that? Be perfect, therefore, as your heavenly Father is perfect' (Matthew 5:47–48). Those are strong words from our Lord. 'God so loved the world' and so should we. And not from a distance either, but face to face. This has enormous repercussions for evangelism.

At the time of writing, I am the chair of the Evangelism Commission of the Conseil national des évangéliques de France (the CNEF or, in English, the French National Council of Evangelicals). As part of our work on the topic of evangelism on behalf of all the churches affiliated with the CNEF, we organized a series of three surveys.

The first one was internal. We asked all the pastors of these churches a raft of questions about their views on evangelism in today's France and on their practices. In particular, we asked the question, 'What are the best means of evangelism today?' to which 87.6% of the respondents replied, 'Building relationships with non-Christians.' In answer to another question, 'What training do you think is necessary for church members?' 75.3% of respondents chose, 'How to build relationships with non-Christians.'

In one sense, that is surprising. Why do we need training for something so obvious? Do a young couple who have just become engaged to be married need training to tell their friends their good news? Do any of us need training to talk about our favourite films or sports teams?

I think that there could be several reasons why Christians find it hard to talk about their faith. One reason might be that they are no longer enthralled to be Christians. This is why the spiritual aspect of revitalisation is important. Another reason may be that they fear that communicating their Christian beliefs is too problematic in today's spiritual climate. This is why the societal and contextual dimension of revitalisation is important. In some cultures, there may also be a feeling of embarrassment about talking about personal things such as faith in God. It may be that some Christians have grown up thinking that evangelism is the responsibility of evangelists preaching from a pulpit or a stage, or that evangelism is a technique to be learnt with a diagram to show people before asking them to make 'a decision for Christ'.

In order to understand the findings of our first survey more clearly, the CNEF commissioned a follow-up study to be carried out by the BVA Group, a well-known professional survey company. This was done according to the method of quotas used in political surveys, for example, bearing in mind variables such as sex, age, social class, region and place of residence (i.e., city, town or country).

We surveyed these people – most of them non-Christians – to understand their feelings about evangelism and to answer the question, 'How would you like to be evangelized?' Of course we did not word it that way. We actually asked, 'If you wanted to find out about a religion, what would you prefer to do?'

The survey company reached this conclusion in their report for the CNEF: 'The vast majority of French people would prefer to receive their information directly from someone belonging to that faith group.' One figure was especially instructive: '23% would like to talk about it with a believer over a coffee.' Interestingly, this rose to 37% for those aged 18–24 and 49% for those who identified as Muslims in the survey.[1]

For the sake of completeness, I should add that it was possible to choose up to two answers to this question and that the internet was frequently selected as a means of learning about a religion, with 35% of all respondents choosing that option and 45% of those aged 18–24. In contrast, very

---

1 These figures are taken from Sondage sur les Français et les Religions (July 2015).

few people wanted to be approached in the street (2%) or to have information in their letterbox (1%).

The third survey was carried out in 2020 with the help of churches affiliated with the CNEF who identified people who had become Christians in recent years from a completely non-Christian background. These people were asked to fill in an anonymous questionnaire online and the results confirmed our intuitions and the information from the professional survey. It turned out that the most important factor in bringing the person to believe in Jesus as Lord and Saviour had been their relationship with a Christian who was close to them: a friend, a colleague, a neighbour or even a health professional. Almost two-thirds (65%) of respondents mentioned this, though there was no specific question about the first contact. We had, in fact, been looking for other sociological factors and the main one that these converts identified as impressive was the willingness of Christians to listen to their questions and to give clear and relevant answers.

The witness of ordinary believers

God has given evangelists to the church ever since the time of the apostles but, through the centuries, the gospel has been spread mostly by ordinary believers. We see this in the early church. After the martyrdom of Stephen in Acts, we read that, 'On that day a great persecution broke out against the church in Jerusalem, and all except the apostles were scattered throughout Judea and Samaria' (Acts 8:1). Luke insists that this dispersion concerned everyone 'except the apostles'. We then read that, 'Those who had been scattered preached the word wherever they went' (Acts 8:4). The story does not end there. In Acts 11:19–21, we see that the same ordinary people who had been scattered went as far as Phoenicia, Cyprus and Antioch and even began to speak to the Greeks to tell them the good news about the Lord Jesus. We also see that a good number believed.

'By this everyone will know that you are my disciples, if you love one another' (John 13:35).

Jesus said that this was how people would know that we are his disciples. So it should be something visible. When people see a community of Christians, they should see people who love and support one another and who trust God with all the events of their lives. In fact, there are very few other places in society where such mixed gatherings exist – male and female, different age groups (i.e., children, young people, families or seniors), different temperaments and social classes and people of different ethnic origins. The church is known as the body of Christ. When Jesus walked the earth, people could see God walking among them, but a community of Christians is the only way that God is 'visible' today. Two Bible verses illustrate this. In John, we read that, 'No one has ever seen God, but the one and only Son, who is himself God and is in the closest relationship with the Father, has made him known' (John 1:18). Then we read the same words, 'No one has ever seen God,' for a second time in 1 John 4:12. This time, the means of making him visible is the same test that Jesus gave in John's Gospel: 'if we love one another, God lives in us' (1 John 4:12).

In one sense, this is jumping the gun because so many people around us have never been present with a group of Christians to have seen this love. This means that we must make sure that we also love our neighbours. Paul emphasizes this in his first letter to the Thessalonians:

> May the Lord make your love increase and overflow for each other *and for everyone else*, just as ours does for you.
> (1 Thessalonians 3:12, my emphasis)

> Make sure that nobody pays back wrong for wrong, but always strive to do what is good for each other *and for everyone else*.
> (1 Thessalonians 5:15, my emphasis)

In other words, our lifestyle (the way that we live as Christians) must be visible. 'Live such good lives among the pagans that, though they accuse you of doing wrong, they may see your good deeds and glorify God on the day he visits us' (1 Peter 2:12). Some people may feel threatened by this, as Peter says in this verse, but we do it anyway.

That said, our first aim is to love people and to build good relationships with them. Not everyone will become a friend in the deepest sense of the word but we can try to establish a healthy connection with as many people as possible. Within society, we can identify four relational networks: family, our workplace or place of education, the community where we live and our leisure time and friendships. All of us are part of one or more of these networks. These are the places where we meet people and where we are called to live for Christ. The New Testament has a great deal to say about family relationships and our motivations at work, but I want to emphasize the link between these relationships and the ways that we can share the gospel. Our friendships must be genuine. We cannot treat people as evangelistic projects. If our care for them is genuine, then we will desire for them to know Jesus too. To love someone means to desire their well-being, which covers their material, emotional and spiritual needs. We want to help them to the best of our ability, encourage their emotional flourishing and share the gospel.

Learning to connect

As we saw in the surveys, we have to learn how to connect with people. Two New Testament passages can help us here. Let's turn to Peter first:

> Who is going to harm you if you are eager to do good? . . . But in your hearts revere Christ as Lord. Always be prepared to give an answer to everyone who asks you to give the reason for the hope that you have. But do this with gentleness and respect.
> (1 Peter 3:13, 15)

What do we have to learn? How to do good, how to honour Christ and how to answer people who ask us questions. This will very often require knowledge of the Bible and of today's culture (which we will come to in the next chapter).

The second passage comes from the apostle Paul: 'Be wise in the way you act towards outsiders; make the most of every opportunity. Let your conversation be always full of grace, seasoned with salt, so that you may know how to answer everyone' (Colossians 4:5–6). What do we have to learn here? How to build a relationship with an 'outsider' (this is the New Testament vocabulary for a non-Christian); how to watch out for opportunities to do good and to share the gospel; how to speak in an interesting way (avoiding Christian jargon); how to answer the questions we are asked; and (from the preceding verses) how to pray for open doors to proclaim Christ.

There are very few New Testament instructions on evangelism but these passages give us an excellent guide: answer people's questions. In this way, we are neither being manipulative nor throwing our pearls to pigs (see Matthew 7:6). If people ask, it is because they want to know. However, it must be remembered that the questions posed in our conversations are not always in the interrogative form. A Christian may just respond to another person's statement but we must not be afraid to speak for fear of losing a friendship. 'The mouth speaks what the heart is full of' (Luke 6:45). That is why we need spiritual revitalisation, as we will explain further in chapter 11.

Lesslie Newbigin states:

> What really needs to be said is where the church is faithful to its Lord, there the powers of the kingdom are present and people begin to ask the question to which the gospel is the answer. And that, I suppose, is why the letters of St Paul contain so many exhortations to faithfulness but no exhortations to be active in mission.[2]

I think that it is a slight exaggeration to write, 'no exhortations to be active in mission', because, as we have just seen, we are all sent towards others to love them. But this does pose the question of what will bring people to ask questions. Newbigin believes, as do I, that it is the life of the Christian community. As we have already seen, Jesus taught, 'By this everyone will know that you are my disciples, if you love one another' (John 13:35). Our friends and acquaintances may not wish to come to our church gatherings and see this for themselves. So what do we do? I think that this is where hospitality is so important, just as we saw that it can help to improve relationships among Christians.

Jesus showed us the way. Luke's Gospel contains accounts of eight meals. More than half of them were with people who were not Jesus' disciples:

- Luke 5:27–39, in the home of Levi the tax collector
- Luke 7:36–50, in the home of Simon the Pharisee
- Luke 11:37–54, in the home of another Pharisee
- Luke 14:1–24, in the home of a prominent Pharisee
- Luke 19:1–10, in the home of Zacchaeus

Hospitality was so important that Luke records Jesus saying, 'The Son of Man *came* eating and drinking' (Luke 7:34, my emphasis), which is an interesting parallel to a later saying of Jesus also recorded by Luke:

---

2 Lesslie Newbigin, *The Gospel in a Pluralist Society* (Grand Rapids, MI: Eerdmans, 1989) p. 118.

'The Son of Man *came* to seek and to save the lost' (Luke 19:10, my emphasis).

As we meet with people, as we are invited to their homes and invite them to ours, or as we go out for a drink together, we are revealing ourselves and our values while praying that we can make the Saviour known. Here in Paris, an important part of my outreach is spent in coffee shops chatting with men I have come to know who are in some sense seeking meaning in their lives.

In today's world, there is much loneliness and ignorance about what the Bible teaches and a bias against 'religion'. For the most part, Christians do not have easy access to the mainstream media, but one thing that we can offer is unconditional love for those around us. Our prayer is that they will open up to God's love and seek salvation.

THE SOCIETAL DIMENSION OF REVITALISATION

I have become all things to all people so that
by all possible means I might save some.
1 Corinthians 9:22

We hear them declaring the wonders of God
in our own tongues.
Acts 2:11

A small town near Manchester, UK

Saturday breakfast. Jane was sleeping in but Tom had decided to get up and have a peaceful breakfast. He had once read a book in which the author had claimed that the key to a successful marriage was not having breakfast together. Maybe that was an exaggeration, but he did like a lazy, peaceful breakfast on a Saturday. All through the week, the alarm rang and he had to drag himself out of bed to get ready for work. For a Christian, Sundays were not a day of rest either – at least not if you defined 'rest' as getting up late.

Tom put the kettle on and slipped a slice of bread into the toaster. A few seconds later, there was a bang and blue smoke rose from the toaster. There was an acrid smell and Tom knew that he wouldn't be having toast for breakfast that morning. He managed to find some cereal and settled down with a magazine as the sun poured in through the window.

When Jane finally woke up, Tom explained what had happened. After she had had a cup of tea, she opened her computer and started looking online for the best deal for a new toaster. Tom knew that she quite enjoyed looking for bargains on the internet so he left her to it and went out to the garden to look after his vegetable patch.

Jane scrolled through the different sites where she usually made her online purchases. She found a good model but the user comments were very negative: 'I bought this model but it broke only two months later,' or, 'It didn't toast the bread very evenly.' Then she found another toaster that she liked and the consumer comments were much more encouraging: 'Very attractive, modern design,' with, 'the possibility of varying the toasting time'. One user said, 'I've had a toaster of this make for fifteen years and I've never had a problem, so I'm going for the same manufacturer.'

An hour later, Tom came in for a cup of coffee and asked Jane if she had found what she was looking for.

'Yes,' she said. 'And I've ordered it. It should arrive by Tuesday at the latest.'

Tom was amazed. 'How do you manage to choose so quickly?' he asked.

'It's easy,' Jane replied. 'I look at what other users think and follow their recommendations.'

Tom was pensive. He liked to connect ideas together and now it was as though a light had come on in his head. 'Of course, Jane. That's it! We keep mentioning evangelism, especially as we've been talking about changes in our church. But it's all so abstract! As you said, we need recommendations. People need to see what it means to be a Christian. Not just as an idea but in real life.

It's a bit like those influencers on the internet. We have to show people around us by our lives that faith in Jesus is a real option, even today.'

Jane smiled. 'From a toaster to evangelism. That's so typical of you, Tom.'

A village in central Romania

It was a Monday evening near the end of term. The twins had virtually no homework so the whole Constantinescu family had watched a television documentary about global warming.

When Ana turned off the television, Alexandru turned to his father and asked, 'Dad, what does the Bible teach about looking after our environment?'

There was a moment of stunned silence. Stefan had never had any teaching on this subject during his studies at the seminary. He hadn't read any books on the subject either. But he was unwilling to admit his ignorance to his son, so he answered in a very non-committal way, 'That's a big question, Alexandru.'

Teenagers don't like it when they don't get a proper answer, so Alexandru insisted. 'At school we have lessons on ecology and biodiversity as well as global warming. Some of my friends are passionate about this and have even been on marches in Bucharest to get our government to invest more in sustainable development. It's almost like a religion for some of them. And they're very frightened about the future. One of my friends asked me what I thought as a Christian – they all know my Dad's a pastor – and I had to admit that I didn't have a clue.'

Not to be outdone, Alexandru's twin brother Mihai latched onto another subject. 'Dad, a boy in my class has come out as gay. How should I react to him? I don't think I've ever heard a sermon on this in church. At school some of the kids are militant about these issues. They say that Romania is a very conservative country compared to Western Europe and that the church just repeats what society thinks. Do you think that's true? What does the Bible say? At catechism we were taught that the Bible is our final authority.'

Stefan decided that honesty was the best policy. 'You're right. If we want to show how important the gospel is, we've got to be able to show that it's credible in all areas of our lives. Maybe it's not a problem for the older folks, but I agree that the world is changing and you can't stop ideas from spreading on social media or being talked about on television. But I just don't think that I'm capable of giving good answers at the moment. I'm sorry.'

Ana wanted to protect her husband. 'It's not your fault, dear. You weren't trained to give answers to those questions. But I wonder if they offer intensive courses at the seminary that you could attend. I'm sure that the church could finance you going to Bucharest for a week. In other jobs employees have in-service training. Why couldn't you?'

Alexandru was learning English at school and thought that he could find some useful material on the internet that they could discuss at the youth group. Not to be outdone by his twin, Mihai suggested that they invite a visiting speaker. 'Can't they send us one of those people you keep talking about from your European Leadership Forum?'

Stefan was happy that his boys were making some practical suggestions. He needed to bring this up with the newly formed revitalisation team. Where was all of this taking them? Would they get out of their depth and drown? He was a little fearful but determined to keep moving towards what the ELF mentoring team called 'a healthy church', one that loved God and loved people in its cultural context. Having seen the need, there was no turning back, even if it hurt to admit his own shortcomings.

9

The societal dimension of revitalisation: plausibility

Aim: to improve the contextualization of the church

As I have already written several times, a healthy church is a fellowship of believers, redeemed through the gospel, who are learning to love God with all their heart, with all their soul, with all their mind, with all their strength and to love people in their cultural context.

Culture is an all-encompassing reality. The United Nations Educational, Scientific and Cultural Organization (UNESCO) defines it in this way: 'The whole complex of distinctive spiritual, material, intellectual and emotional features that characterize a society or a social group. It includes not only the arts and letters, but also modes of life, the fundamental rights of the human being, value systems, traditions and beliefs.'[1] That includes nearly everything you can think of.

I believe that the diversity of cultures is as much part of God's plan as the varieties of flowers, birds or animals in the world. In his speech to the Areopagus, Paul says, 'From one man he made all the nations, that they should inhabit the whole earth; and he marked out their appointed times in history and the boundaries of their lands' (Acts 17:26).

Culture gives us a sense of identity. We are what we are because of the history, geography and customs of the place where we live. For example,

---

1 This quotation is taken from the Mexico Declaration on Cultural Policies adopted at the World Conference on Cultural Policies, Mexico City, 26 July – 6 August 1982. You can read the full text at "Mexico City Declaration on Cultural Policies."

the attitude to religion in France goes back to 'the wars of religion' in the sixteenth century and the French Revolution of 1789, which still influences debates today. Geography also influences us because if you live in a mountainous area it may be difficult to go from one village to another and if you live by the sea (as two of my children do) you are very aware of the pattern of the tides. In addition, culture influences us because there are certain things that you can or cannot do in relation to others. An awareness of the local culture can make life simpler, for example, because you know how to greet someone in an appropriate way or you know the acceptable time to visit a friend. Being culturally aware means that a church might look different in various countries or even in various regions of the same country. We have to move away from the 'one-size-fits-all' mentality and dare to be creative. I remember hearing of a church that organized an Alpha Course at eleven o'clock on a Sunday evening. Although it sounds strange, there was a good reason for the decision. It was a Chinese church in a European capital city and they were aiming to reach the waiters who worked in Chinese restaurants after their evening shift.

But there is another side to the story. Culture also contributes to our mental representation of the world. We come to see some things as 'normal' and other things as 'strange'. It can even come to the point where there is confusion between culture and nature. What is perceived as natural may simply be the way that something is done in a particular culture but the people in that culture begin to think that it is universally true. Peter Berger, an American sociologist, coined the expression 'plausibility structures' to convey this.[2] Social arrangements and institutions (for example, schools, the media, the government or the judicial system) make a certain way of thinking appear self-evident. This has a great relevance to our communication of the gospel. More and more people see ethical choices as the reflection of cultural influences and nothing to do with human nature, for example, the belief that your gender is your choice. A famous French philosopher, Simone de Beauvoir, wrote many years ago, 'One is not born, but rather becomes a woman.'[3] There is some truth in this. Socialization from an early age can create

---

2 See Peter Berger, *The Sacred Canopy: Elements of a Sociological Theory of Religion* (New York: Anchor, 1990).

3 Simone de Beauvoir, *The Second Sex*, trans. Constance Borde (New York: Vintage, 2010) p. 330.

expectations about what is normal for your role in life. In the past, some Christians have fallen into the trap of thinking that certain lifestyles are more 'Christian' than others (for example, the attitude that 'a woman's place is in the home'). However, we should not fall into the opposite trap of thinking that gender is completely fluid. There is considerable pressure in the world today from the 'plausibility structures' in European society to shape the culture in such a way that nonbiblical ways of thinking become normal. This has considerable consequences for evangelism and even for our growth as Christians in faith and obedience to God. This example (and there may be many others within your context) shows clearly why the second 's' of the revitalisation process has to be the societal dimension.

Our changing cultural context

It is important to understand how people view life today. I believe that Europeans have begun to lose the cultural presuppositions on which the edifice of our society was built. They have weakened our society by rejecting its Judeo-Christian foundations. To put it another way, many people today still seem to appeal to the same standards of behaviour and thinking that they did in the past. Whether they recognize it or not, these values come from Christianity,[4] which they no longer wish to embrace. It is like pulling out a tree by the roots and still expecting it to bear fruit.

We can see three consequences of this loss of values when we look at people's lives today. First, a considerable number of Europeans have lost their belief in the existence of truth. For example, you hear people say, 'That's my truth,' or, 'I need to be true to myself.' People only trust themselves. What they feel inside themselves is more authentic, more real and truer than any of the objective arguments that have become suspect in a 'post-truth' world where fake news and conspiracy theories flourish. The dangers of this approach are only too clear. It can result in an egocentric self-sufficiency where people tend to attribute their success to their own qualities (internal causes) and their failures to factors that do not depend

---

4 I recommend two books for further reading on this theme: Vishal Mangalwadi, *The Book that Made Your World: How the Bible Created the Soul of Western Civilization* (Nashville, TN: Thomas Nelson, 2012) and Tom Holland, *Dominion: The Making of the Western Mind* (London: Abacus, 2020).

on them (external causes) in order to maintain a positive self-image. This creates a highly fragile sense of self and opens the door to the feeling of being a victim. While we ought to care for those who are vulnerable (for example, due to discrimination, past trauma or mental health), there still needs to be room in our culture to discuss ideas and challenge one another. As Christians, we are not willing to be silent with the gospel. The only real examples of civil disobedience in the New Testament are when the apostles were told not to speak or teach in the name of Jesus (Acts 4:18–20; 5:27–32) and they responded by affirming, 'We must obey God rather than human beings!' (Acts 5:29).

Second, a considerable number of Europeans no longer believe that life has the overarching meaning that historically gave us the idea of progress. For many today, the only meaning in life is individual. It is linked to what we find in our relationships, work or whatever is important to us. For several centuries, Europeans were convinced that things were improving, that society was developing into something better than their forefathers knew. Today, there is a return to the notion of cyclical time with the idea of coming apocalyptic catastrophes. Without denying the need to work to reduce climate change and protect biodiversity, for example, it often seems to me that the main motivation of many Europeans is anxiety and fear rather than hope. Christians believe that there is a direction to history. God is building his kingdom here and now for eternity so there is real meaning to life both in this world and in the next.

Third, a considerable number of Europeans have lost any objective basis for the essential dignity of human beings (which comes from being made in the image of God) by grounding it in human autonomy. The older Christian conception is fading away and being replaced by a constructed identity conferred by others, by society or by oneself (which is often a virtual identity constructed via the internet). Instead of trying to change the world, they try to change their own personal inner world. There are whole shelves of self-help books in supermarkets and bookshops to illustrate this. People are trying to live as happily as possible in the here and now so everyone should be tolerant of your personal choice just as you should accept the choices of others. People talk about their right to try to protect themselves from being victims of what others do or think and set up lobbies to make sure that legislation is enacted to satisfy their desires. In fact, in our hyperindividualistic culture, many people see any constraints on autonomy, even healthy ones, as oppressive.

But, as we have already seen, humans have been created in the image of God (Genesis 1:27) and two things are striking in today's context:

1 Human beings have great intrinsic value.
2 We are either male or female, and that is true for every cell of our body. I acknowledge that some people have intersex conditions and they should be shown care and dignity, but this does not invalidate the fundamentally binary nature of sex.

Christians think that this gives every human being dignity and identity and affirms that the desire to care for the oppressed is a good and worthy aspiration.

The fact is that, in the eyes of many Europeans, Christianity has been tried for centuries but is no longer relevant in today's world. Because Christianity has been rejected, evangelism today is as difficult as introducing someone to their ex-wife as a possible future partner. In other words, we cannot go on imagining that the ways in which we did things and the way that we explained things in our churches fifty years ago will have an impact on people today.

In short, because we live in societies that are built less and less on Christian foundations, we should never allow ourselves to be married to the spirit of the age, otherwise the church would soon be a widow as one way of thinking succeeded another. We march to the beat of a different drum: that of God's revelation in Scripture. But (and this is a big but) that does not justify a total disconnect with the world around us because of the vast changes in society over the past few years.

Churches need to help Christians live their lives in the contemporary world in order to understand today's challenges and temptations in light of the Bible's teaching. They must also help Christians to understand the rest of the population and better communicate the gospel to them in a way that they will understand – and which sounds like good news. In other words, we need to understand our society both for the sake of the spiritual health of Christians and for the sake of evangelism. The two things are intertwined.

We are now in a better position to see why there is a disconnect between churches and many of the people around us. They are suspicious of ideas that they feel are being imposed on them. They are more interested in what is real, in what works and in what will help them to have a better life. How can they have peace of mind? Does prayer work? In time, they might more easily understand that sin is not primarily a moral category but something that destroys relationships. This is not to deny biblical teaching but to see where we can connect with people in the first instance as they watch us live as individuals and as a gathered church.

We need to live out and demonstrate a reality that is external to us. Let's show a rootedness in the human condition – in history, in nature, in God – instead of just looking inside ourselves for meaning. In other words, the messenger precedes the message. People are more likely to consider looking at the message when the messenger lives a plausible and consistent life, just as you are more likely to buy some household equipment or go to a particular restaurant if other people rate them highly and recommend them.

The inescapable need to contextualize

We cannot avoid contextualization. Today's society is neither wholly good nor wholly bad, but it is the water in which we must catch our fish. This is how the celebrated Lausanne Covenant expresses it in its Article 10, Evangelism and Culture:

> The development of strategies for world evangelisation calls for imaginative pioneering methods. Under God, the result will be the rise of churches deeply rooted in Christ and closely related to their culture. Culture must always be tested and judged by Scripture. Because men and women are God's creatures, some of their culture is rich in beauty and goodness. Because they are fallen, all of it is tainted with sin and some of it is demonic. The gospel does not presuppose the superiority of any culture to another, but evaluates all cultures according to its own criteria of truth and righteousness, and insists on moral absolutes in every culture. Missions have, all too frequently, exported with the gospel an alien culture, and churches have sometimes been in bondage to culture rather than to Scripture. Christ's evangelists must humbly seek to empty them-selves of all but their personal authenticity in order to become the servants of others, and churches must seek to transform and enrich culture, all for the glory of God. (Mark 7:8–9, 13; Genesis 4:21–22; 1 Corinthians 9:1–23; Philippians 2:5–7; 2 Corinthians 4:5)

This article is an appeal to Christians to take culture into account, but it also draws our attention to an inherent difficulty: we need to be closely related to culture but at the same time rooted in Christ. Drawing the line for how much adaptation we are called to make will always be a subject of debate among Christians. Paul deals with this question at length in Romans 14 and 1 Corinthians 8 – 10 using the categories of weak and strong consciences. How much of culture do we accept for the sake of the communication of the gospel and which parts of culture do we reject as being contrary to a Christian way of life? Although we need debate, the need for cultural adaptation cannot be denied. In the next chapter, we will take a further look at how this applies to the revitalisation of a local church.

I wrote in chapter 2 that non-Christians need to see that our faith is plausible. Demonstrating the plausibility of our faith has to be the first stage of our apologetics as we pray that people will move from realizing that faith in Jesus is plausible to seeing it as desirable and then as credible. In other words: 'This seems to work. I must check it out,' to, 'I like it,' to (even in today's culture), 'Is it true?' In using the word 'plausibility', my aim in church revitalisation is that Christian faith should not be dismissed automatically before people have considered it properly and that people should move beyond their indifference as they see that our faith is relevant to our (and their) lives. As our beautiful French language puts it, that it can *entrer dans le champ du possible*, meaning 'enter into the realm of what is feasible'.

Living lives that show the plausibility of the gospel

How can we do this? One method is the way that we use the Bible and live out its realistic message in today's fallen world. We find many things in the Bible that make sense in a postmodern world and that serve as bridges towards our culture. For example, the Bible contains all sorts of literary styles, foremost among them the narrative. People love stories (for example, television series, movies, video games, books or comics) and learn from seeing how other people live their lives. Stories are not linear. They deal with the awkward realities of life in a fallen world. A person today is more likely to be interested in how we cope with these realities than in any pretension that we have all the answers (and, in any case, we do not). But we do know enough to trust God with our lives and hold on to our living hope. We live in the true story of God's good creation, followed by the fall and then by redemption in Jesus. His life, death and resurrection is the basis of our salvation, and the reason for our confidence in God.

So what would a non-Christian see as they began to get to know us at home, at work or in our leisure activities? What would help them to see that our faith works and make them want to ask us questions as they begin to look into this 'option'? What are some of the positives of being a Christian?

- We have a new, real and lasting identity as God's children (see Romans 8:16). We do not have to construct our identity or use secondary things (such as nationalism or gender) to give us this identity.
- We have become part of a worldwide family: the community of God's people.
- Belonging to this community, we can experience God's love and build relationships that will go on forever.
- We do not need to look to self-help books for our deepest needs. Our reading of the Bible and the time we spend together in our local community of God's people will allow us to examine our lives without fear as God works a slow but radical change in our characters in fellowship with the Creator himself.
- We have good reasons to work for justice and mercy on earth because we know that they reflect God's heart.
- We can know great contentment as we wholeheartedly thank God for what we have rather than dwelling on what we wish that we had.
- We are not totally at a loss in the face of suffering since we can trust in God, call on his help and be assured that suffering will not have the last word.
- We can have complete confidence in the face of death.

As we live these things out in today's context, we pray that people will see that our faith is coherent, consistent, and that it gives real meaning to life – both the big picture of the meaning of life and the details of day-to-day living, both through our individual lives and through our lives as part of a community of believers.

Chapter 9

Tim Keller puts it like this:

If Christianity has begun to make emotional and cultural sense they may listen to a sustained discussion of why it makes logical and rational sense. By 'emotional sense' I mean that Christianity must be shown to fill holes and answer questions and account for phenomena in the personal, inward, heart realm. By 'cultural sense' I mean that Christianity must be shown to have the resources to powerfully address our social problems and explain human social behaviour. Only if their imagination is captured will most people *give a fair hearing* to the strong arguments for the truth of Christianity. Let's appeal to heart and imagination as well as to reason as we speak publicly about our faith in Jesus.[5]

---

5 Tim Keller, "Pascal's Method for Presenting the Christian Faith," www.thegospelcoalition. org/article/pascals-method-for-presenting-the-christian-faith (my emphasis). In his article Tim Keller is referring to a quotation from Pascal which you will find in the scenario 'A small town near Manchester, UK' before chapter 15 of this book.

A city in the west of France

The Bible art exhibition had been a great success. It had been well publicized in the local paper and the mayor had come to the official opening to make a short speech before drinking a glass of champagne and nibbling some savoury biscuits with the organizers. The artist was delighted to have met with such appreciative visitors. In short, the event had helped to put the church on the map and about fifty men and women unconnected to the church had passed through its doors for the first time.

Guillaume and Valérie thought that the time was now ripe to ask to meet Denis (the pastor) and the leadership team to take things a step further. They agreed.

The following Tuesday evening, after a few minutes of small talk, Denis said, 'Well, let's get down to business. I know there's something you want to share with us this evening.'

Guillaume cleared his throat and launched straight in. 'Yes. Valérie and I have a suggestion to make, but of course we need your approval and support. I guess that's why we're here.' Guillaume didn't feel quite as comfortable as he did when he made a presentation at work. After the meeting, he explained to Valérie that he had suddenly become aware of how much was at stake and he hadn't wanted to make a false move. But he had seen the leadership group making encouraging signs for him to come out with what he had to say, so he had continued. 'Do you remember one of the ideas expressed at the learning community that we should have special Sunday evening services aimed at young professionals like us?' Guillaume hesitated for a second. 'Valérie and I would be happy to organize them and we know that the new couple who have just started attending the church, Thomas and Myriam, would be happy to join us in this venture. We were thinking of starting with a monthly meeting. And of course it wouldn't stop us from coming to the church on Sunday morning,' Guillaume hastened to add. He wanted to reassure the leadership that this wouldn't be a sort of breakaway group.

Michel, one of the founders of the church who had been the same age as Guillaume and Valérie when the church had been planted, gave them a quizzical look. 'Do you mean that there's a problem with our morning services?' he asked a bit gruffly.

Valérie jumped in, 'No, not all. But a lot of people our age just don't get up on Sunday morning until they go out for a brunch with their friends. Even if we invited them, they wouldn't come.'

Case study

Guillaume, emboldened by Valérie's reply, added that because of their friends' busy lives, they would be attracted to a quieter, more reflective time together than was possible on a Sunday morning with the presence of so many children. He bit his tongue so as not to add that the 'state-of-the-art' worship music on a Sunday morning was not what their friends were looking for.

Valérie smiled and said that anyone from the leadership team would be welcome to come along and see for themselves and that she and Guillaume would be thankful for their input.

Sylvia, a middle-aged woman who worked in a local bank, said she would love to take part in these evening services. She went on, 'As a single woman, I must admit that I'm often distracted by the noise of the children in the morning service. Don't get me wrong – I'm pleased that they come with their parents, but maybe it's time to offer something different. After all, why should church be the only place in the modern world that still thinks that one size fits all? I vote we give it a try!'

10

The societal dimension of revitalisation: adaptability

Aim: to improve the contextualization of the church

'I have become all things to all people so that by all possible means I might save some' (1 Corinthians 9:22). Those are the very words that Paul used to explain contextualization, though he did not use that particular term. In the verses that come just before this statement, he explains how he tries to be like a Jew when he is with Jews and like a Gentile ('not under the law', see 1 Corinthians 9:20) when he is with Gentiles. He practised what he preached.

There is a very interesting sequence of events in the middle of Acts when Paul preaches to three very different audiences. First, in Acts 13, he preaches the Messiah to his fellow Jews in the synagogue in Pisidian Antioch. He quotes a range of Old Testament prophecies and applies them to Jesus, calling for repentance and faith in order to be right with God.

Next, in Acts 14, Paul is in Lystra, situated in a rural area where the inhabitants believed in the Greek gods. Paul explains that there is one creator who gives them good harvests, who provides them with plenty of food and who fills their hearts with joy. This is very down to earth. In fact, Paul does not quote the Bible here but he does appeal to the people to turn from their worthless idols to the living God.

Then, in Acts 17, we find Paul in Athens, the intellectual capital of the Roman Empire. In his speech to the Areopagus, he uses abstract language: 'In him we live and move and have our being' (Acts 17:28). I wonder if the farmers in Lystra would have understood this! Paul quotes their own poets but he does not mention the Bible as such. However, he does lead up to a call to change with the words, 'In the past God overlooked such ignorance, but now he commands all people everywhere to repent' (Acts 17:30).

What conclusions can we draw when we look at Europe today? If churches are to be revitalised, we have to know how people think so that our words have a real impact. That is why it is a good starting point to look at the upcoming generations not only because we want to reach out to them but also because this helps us to see the way that society is moving as a whole. Any description of a 'generation' should be approached with caution since we cannot base our perception of thought and behaviour on the sole criterion of the period in which someone was born. Nevertheless, a generation is, in one sense, all the people who are living on earth at one time. Everyone is influenced by the way in which society is evolving and looking at the characteristics of the generations that are growing up in the twenty-first century is a good way of understanding the ways in which we need to contextualize in today's society.

Understanding younger generations

I have observed a few characteristics in the upcoming generations.

They are hyperconnected

- Technology is an extension of their brain.
- They can have great capacity for adaptation as they are often open-minded and enterprising.
- On social media, they may try to manage their image to perfection.
- It can be difficult to channel their attention, as they are always hopping from one screen to another and not concentrating on any one thing for long.
- They are less likely to feel geographically rooted because they can access information and contact each other from anywhere and at any time.
- They are consumers.

They are relational

- Their friends and family are very important to them.
- They want to work in partnership rather than submit to authority.
- They learn interactively.
- However, many have had absolutely no contact with a church.

Their attitude to work can also be very revealing. I have observed that younger people often want their work to be fun, innovative and ethical (especially as far as ecology is concerned). They want a boss who will listen to them and who has a direct relationship with them based on honesty. Many want a certain degree of freedom to be creative and delight in multitasking to avoid boredom. They may enjoy working as a team (coworking is a popular idea) and feel the need to celebrate successes together. The old proverb, 'All work and no play makes Jack a dull boy,' holds true for this generation, so they will often want to talk about things other than their job and to have enough time to enjoy themselves away from work.

How does this affect church life?

There are a few consequences of today's lifestyle.

First, church is seen as a leisure activity, sociologically speaking. The idea of attending church as a weekly 'duty' comes from a previous generation and this is not the way that people think today. The motivation for attending church is community, meeting people and being with friends. Why make the effort to attend church services? The answer is in the added value of true fellowship and of truly sharing our lives. I should add that growth in spiritual maturity will lead people to grow in commitment as they come to understand more about what it means to be part of the body of Christ together, with a desire to serve others without expecting anything in return.

Second, people have access to thousands of videos of preachers and Christian musicians online and this means that a local church has to help members to be discerning about what they see. Just as teachers know that the pupils in their classes will investigate what they are teaching by going online, nearly everyone today has the reflex of going to their screen for information and using social media to exchange ideas with others.

Third, there may be times when we have to reconsider when we meet together. What are the best times to meet during the week and on Sundays? There are so many other leisure activities on offer and these can clash with church services. If children play sports, their matches may well be on Sunday morning (at least, this is our experience in France). So do people deprive their children of sport and deprive themselves of meeting other parents at the matches and building relationships that could open doors to the gospel? Some churches now meet on Sunday afternoon to avoid the scheduling conflict, but this may be at the expense of other priorities (for example, visiting grandparents). Maybe we should think in terms of a plurality of offers such as several different types of Sunday meetings at different times according to the needs of the congregation. Sometimes churches can fear that this will harm the unity of the fellowship. This is understandable but it all depends on the model that people have in their mind. Unity is not the same thing as uniformity. After all, cinemas today have several screens and schools have different classes but they still have an identity as a cinema or a school. This approach to church life is not intended to foster a consumer mindset or to underplay the unity of the church. There are various ways for the whole church to gather on certain occasions and, though a church may well propose various alternative approaches to God, unity can still be possible on other levels such as home groups, special events at Christmas or Easter, or involvement in other church activities such as humanitarian projects with people who would usually attend a different service. It is the biblical norm for Christians to meet together regularly but each church must consider prayerfully the best way to encourage this in today's world.

Fourth, going further down this path, we have to accept that society is very diverse today, and it is more and more difficult to reach a consensus. There are differences between generations in terms of their pattern of activity during a day, there is a growing awareness that a particular musical style cannot appeal to everyone and there are more and more Christians from Africa, Asia and South America living in Europe who have their own traditions of worship and church. In addition, there are more and more Christians who have cut off contact with other Christians and who no longer attend church, often because they do not feel that they are being encouraged in their walk with Christ in today's world because of the way that their church functions. The topics that their contemporaries are talking about (such as global warming) are not mentioned in sermons or Bible studies and they are not being helped to explain Christian ethics in a way that communicates with the people in their environment.

Allow me to give you an example of how this worked out in our church in central Paris. The church has been in existence for over a century but the urban context leads inevitably to a high turnover of people attending the church. Students finish their courses and move on. Young married couples need a bigger flat to bring up a family so they move to the suburbs or to the provinces because the flats in central Paris are so expensive. The church has always had to keep adapting but one thing never changed: there was always one service on a Sunday and that was in the morning. As we looked at the lifestyle of young Parisians, we came to the conclusion that we needed to launch an evening service as well. There were several reasons for this decision:

- A lot of young people go to bed very late on Saturday evening because they are with their friends. A non-Christian would be unlikely to come to a Sunday morning service and a Christian would not feel so free to be with their friends if they had to get up on Sunday morning to go to church.
- Many young people go away from Paris at weekends either for leisure activities or to see their parents but they return by Sunday evening to prepare for the next week.
- Sunday evening is the time of the week when many young people feel lonely and depressed after a pleasant weekend and they may be looking for company before returning to work on Monday morning.

Two other factors encouraged us to start Sunday evening worship:

- Our church building is quite small (property is expensive in Paris) and a second congregation would allow the church to grow.
- This would be an opportunity to experience worship differently.

The people who come to the evening service sit in a circle (I cannot claim that hundreds of people attend) and we have a different form of worship each week. I remember one girl telling me that she wanted to be surprised each week by what we had prepared. She did not want routine. First – and it often amazes audiences when I recount this story – we only sing once a month. We call it our 'vintage service' and have singing and preaching like in the morning service, except that we try to be more contemplative in our choice of music. This helps us to find time for other ways of worshipping God on other Sundays. It also helps non-Christians to feel more at ease. We have found in our culture that non-Christians have no problem with us praying or reading the Bible but they are embarrassed when we sing (should they stand or sit, sing, pretend to sing or be silent because they do not believe the words?). On some Sundays, we then have a more meditative service, often based on a famous painting of a Bible story. We often use films because audiovisuals are the language of today. We help people to understand the Bible by showing Christian films and comparing what we see to the biblical texts. We also show extracts from secular films,[1] many of which explore biblical themes. We invite speakers to come, we interview them and have questions from the floor on topics such as being a Christian at work, secularism, marriage, science and faith, Islam, ecology, politics and art. We also have special evenings on biblical themes when we try to present these topics in a creative way so that, through the renewal of our intelligence, we will know the one true God and live for his glory.

At every evening service we read the Bible and we have group prayer and sharing. The evening ends with pizza and the conversations continue on an amazing range of subjects in a joyful way. In the New Testament, complaining is highly discouraged but, all too often, Christians can spend their time lamenting the way that society is going. Our gatherings are sometimes very serious but they are often times of rejoicing and celebration as we remember how great God is and give thanks for the life he has given us. 'I rejoiced with those who said to me, "Let us go to the house of the LORD"' (Psalm 122:1). It is difficult to rejoice and celebrate alone.

This example illustrates why we need to contextualize. First, to help Christians live their lives in the contemporary world, to deal with the challenges of today in light of the Bible and to better face up to the subtle temptations of today's culture.

Second, to help Christians to live in a world that is parallel to the rest of the population but not so different that it becomes difficult to build bridges with people around them and identify with the needs of society outside the church. This will enable each of us to reach out to non-believers in a meaningful way. Remember that Paul wrote, 'I have become all things to all people so that by all possible means I might save some' (1 Corinthians 9:22).

I must emphasize that I am in no way offering this as a model for everyone to follow. It works for us in Paris but your context is probably very different. The revitalisation team has to work out the best way

---

1 In many countries you have to pay a copyright fee to conduct public screenings of films. Information about copyright licensing for churches in different countries can be found at www.ccli.com.

forward in your environment. I would also stress that contextualization is not a one-time thing. Churches need to review their situation regularly and start and stop initiatives as their context changes. Adaptability means being responsive to changes both within and beyond the church.

Having encouraged the members to build strong relationships with each other and with non-Christians in today's context, we will now turn to the spiritual dimension of the church. As a healthy church, how can we love God in today's world?

THE SPIRITUAL DIMENSION OF REVITALISATION

Love the Lord your God with all your heart and with all your soul
and with all your mind and with all your strength.
Mark 12:30

A small town near Manchester, UK

Just after he left work, Tom got a text message from Martin asking if he could come round to his house that evening to discuss something. Tom was intrigued. What did Martin want to talk about so urgently? Tom guessed it might be something about the church. He was right.

As soon as Martin appeared at the door, Tom could see that he was excited. Martin was hardly inside their home before he exclaimed, 'I've been asked to lead the service next Sunday morning and I thought we could do it together and start introducing some of the ideas we've been talking about.'

Tom tried to take in what this might entail. What could they do? What things could they change from their normal services? What if they upset someone? How would everyone feel about it?

Martin reassured him. 'We have the support of the elders, Tom. They don't have much experience of church life outside our fellowship. Most of them grew up in this town and they've never seen how things could be done differently. They're keen to see what we can offer. They trust us, Tom!'

Tom was still a bit hesitant. It was one thing to talk about revitalisation but another thing to have the responsibility for changing something.

'We don't have to do anything radical, Tom,' Martin added to alleviate his fears. 'We can just lead the sort of service that we would be happy with in the hope that others will feel the same way. Let's sit down and put some ideas on paper.'

Tom began to warm to the idea. How could they bring a sense of wonder to the congregation? How could they be creative? How could they make the service in some sense unforgettable? And how could they do it in such a way that it wasn't a one-off event but the type of service that could be held week after week?

'First of all, I think there has to be a clear theme,' Tom suggested. 'I don't like it when we go from one thing to another with no clear link between the parts. And if it can be linked to people's day-to-day concerns, that would be even better.'

'That's exactly what I was thinking,' Martin said. 'I thought of basing the service on the words of Jesus, "Do not let your hearts be troubled," in John 14. There's so much anxiety in today's world. If we could trust God and learn not to worry, our lives would be so much better and the people around us couldn't fail to see the difference our faith makes.'

'And there are so many biblical passages that deal with this. We should spend some time listening to them. But we have to get someone to read them well.' Tom was fed up with hearing God's Word recited like a shopping list with no emotion or understanding of the text.

Martin completely agreed. 'I'd thought of that too. Do you know Mrs Connolly? She often sits near the back of the church. She trained as an actress. We could get her to do the Bible reading.'

'Good idea, Martin. And what about using some audiovisual material? Or is that too revolutionary? Only last week I found a short film about how the NASA astronauts celebrated the Lord's Supper after landing on the moon in 1969, just before Neil Armstrong took his first steps on the lunar surface. The first liquid poured on the moon and the first food ever eaten there were the bread and wine of communion. I thought that was fantastic. What do you think about showing the film before we break the bread?'

Their ideas were flowing but Tom and Martin decided not to introduce too many new features at once. There would be time for them all in due course.

When Jane came into the living room to ask if they would like something to drink, she found them praying together. She tiptoed back out. It was a good sign.

A city in the west of France

Soon after Guillaume and Valérie got the green light from the leadership team to start a monthly evening service, they met with their new friends, Thomas and Myriam, to prepare the first one.

Guillaume in particular was a little nervous about doing things right. 'You don't get a second chance to make a first impression,' was a mantra he had often heard at work.

Valérie calmed him down. 'This isn't going to be a show. It's about being real. All we can do is prepare a service that means something to us, to our generation. In any case, I don't think there'll be many of us. And hopefully there'll be some non-Christians who'll be surprised that we're not being very "religious", as they understand it. So there won't be very demanding expectations.'

Thomas and Myriam had recently moved to the city. They had both grown up in Christian homes and needed some help to understand the issues.

Guillaume painted a vivid picture of today's postmodern, post-Christian and post-truth society. 'So you see,' he concluded, 'people make their minds up on the basis of their feelings rather than deciding rationally. We must take that into account in our worship but, at the same time, we must be very careful not to manipulate their feelings! We want others to share our experience of wonder and to see how relevant our faith is to the issues they're facing every day.'

This was so new to Thomas and Myriam that they had no idea how to help in preparing the service but they both felt excited that their friends were on the right track.

'So where do we start?' asked Myriam.

'I've had an idea going round my head for a few days now,' answered Valérie. 'Why don't we build the service around the theme of birds?'

Myriam stared at her. 'Birds?' she muttered.

'Exactly. We live in the city and we see a few birds – mainly pigeons and sparrows – but we could start the service with a string of video clips showing how much diversity there is in creation. Birds come in so many shapes and colours and their songs are so varied and beautiful. We need to stop and admire them, and to do it together so that we can say to each other, "Wow, isn't that fantastic?" That's a way of praising God.'

Thomas got the idea and made a suggestion. 'I'd love to include a clip on the clouds of starlings making patterns in the sky. I once witnessed what they call a murmuration of starlings. It was breathtaking.'

'And then we could spend some time on ecological issues. It's vital not to forget that. It's an inescapable subject for so many people our age,' added Guillaume. 'And we also need to challenge the congregation with some basic biblical teaching.'

'I've been thinking about that, *mon chéri*,' his wife responded. 'I've found two verses we could use. There's one in the Old Testament – Jeremiah 8 – that talks about how the dove, the swift and the thrush observe the time of their migration but the Lord's people don't know what he requires. I think that's all about the conscience we all have but don't always follow. That could also be a way into a non-believer's heart. Then of course we have Jesus' teaching in Matthew 6, about how God watches over the birds of the air so we shouldn't worry about things. No one can add an hour to their life by worrying!'

'I've got a question,' interrupted Myriam. 'Are we going to sing during this service?'

'I've been thinking about that too,' continued Valérie. 'I think it would be better if we watched a video of a suitable song. I know some of the friends I want to invite would be embarrassed to stand up and sing with us.'

'But that doesn't stop us from praying for one another at the end of the service,' Guillaume declared. 'Valérie's two biblical passages would lead us into that nicely. They're relevant to everything we'll be doing during the week. And we can share some prayer requests about the needs and challenges we're facing.'

Thomas was renowned for his healthy appetite so his final suggestion came as no surprise. 'And we could order some pizzas to share together after the service. That would help everyone to feel at ease. That's how we can build friendships with each other.'

A village in central Romania

One evening, Marius the garage owner, the young couple Sofia and Florin, and Grigore the elder met with Stefan and Ana in their home. It was a bit awkward at first because there was some palpable anxiety in the air about the possible repercussions of the decisions they were about to make, but they had agreed to join the group because they were all convinced that the way forward was to encourage the Christians in their church to be salt and light all through the week.

Straight away, they found that they were in agreement that the church needed to encourage and train Christians to build healthy relationships with people in the village and that this included sharing the gospel with them when the opportunity arose. So far, so good. But did they dare put an end to the annual week of evangelism with the invited speaker?

Ana brought in a plate of home-made biscuits and a flask of tea which helped them to relax. After some considerable discussion, they came to the conclusion that it would be better to be positive than to give the impression that change always meant putting a brutal end to things that people were comfortable with.

Florin mentioned the trainer of the village football team. 'His philosophy is that attack is the best form of defence. If we've got the ball in the other team's half, they cannot score.'

Grigore, who was widely read, jumped in and said, 'Exactly. That was what the famous Chinese military commander Sun Tzu wrote in his book *The Art of War*: "Attack is the secret of defence; defence is the planning of an attack."'

Stefan was a bit puzzled about this. How did that apply in his ministry?

Marius came to his rescue. 'I think that you should take the lead and start teaching the congregation about being a scattered church. I bet most of them have never heard the expression, not that that matters. The important thing is to start going down that path. And the sooner the better! Why not launch something this Sunday? If an old car comes into my garage, I'm often tempted to work on something easier but I force myself to get down to it and then do the simpler stuff later in the day.'

Practically minded Ana made the first suggestion. 'Why don't we begin by praying for specific people at the nine o'clock prayer meeting? Our prayers are too vague and sometimes too inward-looking. We could ask everyone to pray for their neighbours, for example.'

'Last week we were looking at Philippians at the ten o'clock Bible study,' Grigore remembered. 'And the timing is superb! I was reading it yesterday. The next bit of Philippians is about the advance of the gospel. Paul recounts how everyone in the palace guard in Rome knew he was in chains for Christ and, as the final greetings in the letter show, some of them became Christians. Because of that, most of the brothers there in Rome were encouraged to speak the Word of God more fearlessly. That's so relevant for us!'

Stefan was beginning to get the message from his group.

'And you could preach on being witnesses all through the week at the eleven o'clock service,' Sofia concluded.

They all prayed for Stefan before saying their goodbyes. He needed it. He would have a lot to share with his ELF church revitalisation mentoring group at their next meeting. Hopefully there would be a lot of positive outcomes to tell them about.

11

The spiritual dimension
of revitalisation

Aim: to improve the spiritual health
of the church

The revitalisation flow chart (see chapter 5) summarizes the spiritual
health of the church in this way:

- the centrality of the gospel
- worshipping God with a sense of wonder, reverence and creativity
  in a way that is also accessible to non-Christians
- earnest prayer

This chapter will take a look at what that can mean as a church undergoes
the revitalisation process in its spiritual dimension. How can we deepen
our spiritual life, our relationship with God and our desire to live a holy
and caring life? How can we keep Christ central in our thoughts and be a
people 'to the praise of his glorious grace', because, 'in him we have
redemption through his blood, the forgiveness of sins' (Ephesians 1:6–7).
And, to be specific, how can the times when we meet together as Christians help us to live this out in an effective way?

Marvel at all that the Lord is
and does and express our
heartfelt praise

This is our primary aim as we meet together as a church: to be filled with
wonder as we realize afresh that there is a mighty and loving Creator and

that we are not alone in an impersonal universe where neither duty nor destiny have any meaning,[1] and to be amazed as we meditate on the depths of God's love in Jesus Christ, his grace in our salvation, and our ultimate and eternal destination. This is how we keep the gospel central in the life of the church and in our own spiritual lives. As we saw in chapter 2, it is so easy for other pet subjects, preoccupations, even obsessions about issues such as styles of worship or questions of ethics in our society to become all-important and lead to the point where a church is in a state of amnesia regarding the gospel itself. The gospel is *the* centre and should lead us to live *sub specie crucis* (meaning 'in light of the cross') and *sub specie aeternitatis* (meaning 'in light of eternity').

This is what Paul prayed for when he wrote to the church in Ephesus: that they would know God better and that the eyes of their hearts would be opened to plumb the depths of the hope to which they had been called – their glorious inheritance and the power of God (see Ephesians 1:17–19). The 'wow factor' we experience when we realize the depth of God's grace is a powerful encouragement to live a holy life: 'The grace of God . . . teaches us to say "No" to ungodliness and worldly passions, and to live self-controlled, upright and godly lives in this present age' (Titus 2:11–12).

It is essential to keep the gospel at the centre of our spiritual lives, but we need to recognize that this does not happen automatically. We have to fight against the twin dangers of legalism (imposing certain ways of doing things) and routine (always doing things in the same way). These are a continual threat to our ability to marvel, which is an inward response to what is said and done during our church services.

It is so important to avoid going through the motions, that is to say, falling into a routine in which nothing unexpected happens. On the other hand, we should always be aware of the opposite danger of manipulating the emotions of a congregation. Of course our emotions are important because they are part of our make-up as human beings. But I believe that the biblical order is not to start with the emotions but with our cognitive faculties. In other words, as we understand things and change our beliefs, our emotions change too. The more we understand the great biblical truths and live by them, the more our emotions

---

1 This is an allusion to a sentence written by the famous atheist scientist Jacques Monod. See Jacques Monod, *Le hasard et la nécessité* (Paris: Éditions du Seuil, 1970).

are aligned with our minds so that we love God with all our heart and with all our soul and with all our understanding. We are right to be wary of uncontrolled and irrational passions, but God gave us feelings as human beings. This means that it is important (and valid) to develop and live out the emotional side of Christianity. This glorifies God.[2] Personally, I am always moved when I see new connections that I had never noticed before.

Preaching and singing are two of the means of grace to open eyes and hearts but we should not be afraid to try different styles of teaching or even different forms of worship services. I have the impression that there is too little local creativity in our evangelical churches. All over the world, the same songs are sung and great preachers are copied (even in terms of walking up and down the stage to preach rather than standing in one place). We can also experiment with different types of music. In our church in Paris, we invited a classical music ensemble to come and sing at our Christmas service. To my surprise, even the children were enthralled listening to medieval Christmas carols.

Preaching and praising God means using words. We should never forget that speech is probably the most miraculous thing that we do every day. Speech is complex. Not even the greatest linguists can explain the origin of language, but I believe that God has given us language so that we can communicate with each other and so that, despite his immense greatness, he can communicate with us. In fact, there is now a second miracle: we have language in written form – whether that is ink on a page or pixels on a screen. This enables knowledge in general and God's revelation in particular to be passed on from generation to generation.

Praising the Lord with words is our active response to the wonder we experience when we contemplate God and his mighty deeds on our behalf. One of the challenges we have in the evangelical world today is that the word 'praise' has become almost synonymous with music and singing and often with a particular style of music, but a Bible-based church should be identifiable by the gospel it preaches and not by the style of music it uses. Furthermore, the word 'praise' does not necessarily imply music. The challenge is to find a good synonym. The best I have

---

2 For further reading on this subject, I recommend Matthew Elliott, *Faithful Feelings: Rethinking Emotion in the New Testament* (London: IVP, 2005).

found is 'to speak highly of God' but that expression does not lend itself to frequent use.

C. S. Lewis expresses it well in his book *Reflections on the Psalms:*

> But the most obvious fact about praise – whether of God or anything – strangely escaped me. I thought of it in terms of compliment, approval, or the giving of honour. I had never noticed that all enjoyment spontaneously overflows into praise . . . The world rings with praise – lovers praising their mistresses, readers praising their favourite poet, walkers praising the countryside, players praising their favourite game – praise of weather, wines, dishes, actors, motors, horses, colleges, countries, historical personages, children, flowers, mountains . . . just as men spontaneously praise whatever they value, so they spontaneously urge us to join them in praising it: 'Isn't she lovely? Wasn't it glorious? Don't you think that magnificent?' The Psalmists in telling everyone to praise God are doing what all men do when they speak of what they care about.[3]

G. K. Chesterton also writes about thanksgiving in his inimitable style:

> You say grace before meals. All right. But I say grace before the concert and the opera, and grace before the play and pantomime, and grace before I open a book, and grace before sketching, painting, swimming, fencing, boxing, walking, playing, dancing and grace before I dip the pen in the ink.[4]

Encouraging this attitude of praise and thanksgiving will spill out into our daily life. What is evangelism if not speaking spontaneously and highly of God to the people around us? The revitalisation team need to think about how to encourage this attitude in the congregation.

In the Greek New Testament, we find the words for 'joy' or 'rejoice' almost 100 times, the word for 'hope' eighty times and the word for 'peace' over forty times. But I have noticed that many Christians are more concerned about the problems of society and they have a rather negative

---

3 C. S. Lewis, *Reflections on the Psalms* (London: Fontana Books, 1967) pp. 79–80. © copyright 1958 CS Lewis Pte Ltd. Extract used with permission.
4 I have been unable to trace where G. K. Chesterton originally wrote this frequently quoted text.

attitude to what is happening around them. This is understandable because, faced with pressure from the media to accept new forms of family and sexuality, Christianity seems to be on the retreat. But the moaners seem to have forgotten that Christians are the new humanity and that Jesus came to bring us abundant life.

Enable each participant to take stock of their life before the Lord

Increasingly, I have noticed one thing about evangelical Christians. We often have a very active approach to life and we like talking, so the one thing that frightens us is silence. As I wrote earlier, I have the highest regard for our capacity as humans to communicate through language but the invitation to, 'Be still, and know that I am God' (Psalm 46:10) is part of our spirituality too. This verse is at the intersection of reflection (our thoughts), desire (our affections) and fellowship (enjoying communion with God). To enjoy God's presence involves knowing who he is through reading Scripture, meditating on these truths and examining our lives to see if our heart's desire is to live in a conscious relationship with this God.

The prophets knew how important it was to have a correct perspective on God and on ourselves. Habakkuk finished a series of prophecies with the words, 'The LORD is in his holy temple; let all the earth be silent before him' (Habakkuk 2:20). Twice, Haggai exhorted the people: 'Give careful thought to your ways' (Haggai 1:5, 7). We find the same thing in the Psalms: 'I have considered my ways and have turned my steps to your statutes' (Psalm 119:59) and 'I remember the days of long ago; I meditate on all your works and consider what your hands have done' (Psalm 143:5).

When we turn to the New Testament, we find that Paul wrote to Timothy, 'Reflect on what I am saying, for the Lord will give you insight into all this' (2 Timothy 2:7) and called on the Philippians to think about whatever is right, pure, lovely and so on (see Philippians 4:8). This should not surprise us because the word 'mind' is found in the verses that are the basis of a healthy church, interconnected with our entire being including heart, soul and strength (see Mark 12:30).

I find it interesting that, in the secular world, the idea of 'mindfulness' is being promoted as a less stressful way of life that teaches you to pay attention to the present moment. The secular world often steals our biblical ideas! However, the secular approach focuses on being non-judgmental and mindful of oneself whereas Christian teaching prioritizes being mindful of God, giving thanks and trusting our unseen God in all circumstances as we think back over his faithfulness.

Because I live in Paris and I like art, I have a card which gives me unlimited access to the Louvre. Unlike the tourists who want to see as many famous paintings as possible in one day, I can spend half an hour looking at just two or three paintings when I go. Thanks to graphic designers and music channels, we are surrounded by art today but do we take the time to look at the packet containing our breakfast cereal or listen with concentration to the music in the background? Usually, we have to go to an art gallery or a concert to give our whole attention to a piece. That is why churches have a great opportunity each week to help our congregations to reflect on important matters by making time during our services and giving people space for reflection. As Christians, we know that (in contrast to secular mindfulness) this space is where the Holy Spirit can work so that our minds focus on what is truly important. Our hearts desire what the Spirit desires and we learn to love what God loves:

> Those who live according to the flesh have their minds set on what the flesh desires; but those who live in accordance with the Spirit have their minds set on what the Spirit desires.
> (Romans 8:5)

The empowerment of the Holy Spirit will enable us to live in light of those things which are truly important:

> So I say, walk by the Spirit, and you will not gratify the desires of the flesh. For the flesh desires what is contrary to the Spirit, and the Spirit what is contrary to the flesh. They are in conflict with each other, so that you are not to do whatever you want. But if you are led by the Spirit, you are not under the law . . . But the fruit of the Spirit is love, joy, peace, forbearance, kindness, goodness, faithfulness, gentleness and self-control . . . Since we live by the Spirit, let us keep in step with the Spirit.
> (Galatians 5:16–18, 22–23, 25)

Get to know God better and live for him in the world in which he has placed us

In Acts 6, the apostles turned over the responsibility of serving food to seven other men, saying that this would enable them (the apostles) to 'give our attention to prayer and the ministry of the word' (Acts 6:4). The reason is clear: these are the ways in which we get to know God better. We need the faithful teaching of the whole Word of God.

I have just finished preaching through Isaiah in my church here in Paris. We looked at one chapter a week, with breaks from time to time to preach through shorter books. It has been a challenge to explain and apply the teaching each Sunday but this entire long book is part of God's Word to us, not just one or two of our favourite chapters. This apostolic teaching should also deal with the very practical issues facing Christians as we live out our lives as salt and light all through the week. This was already the case in the New Testament church. As the gospel spread from Jerusalem throughout the Roman world, the apostles had to address issues that had not arisen when they were teaching the early Jewish believers. For example, in 1 Corinthians, Paul develops a Christian way of thinking about marriage and food sacrificed to idols. Such practical teaching was indispensable to those living in a context where biblical values were not the norm. Paul's arguments in 1 Corinthians 8 – 10 and Romans 14 are paradigms of the way to think through all sorts of issues that arise from surrounding cultures, which we have to face as Christians in our churches and in our daily lives.

Earnest prayer is also a challenge in our Western world. This is partly because of our very full lives. We try to cram more and more into the time available to us, mainly because we are accustomed in our secular society to think that what is measurable and visible is what is most important. If we have a need, there will always be a technical solution, whether it is a visit to the doctor or a trip to the shops to buy the item we need. That is not the case in every country in the world. In addition, we must avoid the danger of being parochial and inward-looking in our prayers. To intercede earnestly for one's own country and for the advance of the gospel across the world can bring a breath of fresh air, or even a blast of reality, to our meetings.

Encourage each other

Community life is a very important dimension of our spiritual health. I have already explored this in chapter 7 when talking about the 'one anothers' of the New Testament. I will not develop this topic further here.

Prepare to live as the 'scattered church' during the rest of the week

We have already noted an obvious fact: Christians spend much more time apart during the week than we spend gathered together. If a believer attends a church service on a Sunday and a couple of other meetings (for example, Bible study or a prayer meeting) during the week, that adds up to about five hours with other Christians out of the 168 hours in a week – only 3% of their life.

And yet we do not stop being Christians during the rest of the week. Paul wrote to the Corinthian church, 'whether you eat or drink or whatever you do, do it all for the glory of God' (1 Corinthians 10:31) and to the Christians in Colossae, 'whatever you do, whether in word or deed, do it all in the name of the Lord Jesus, giving thanks to God the Father through him' (Colossians 3:17).

In its teaching on work and the family, the Bible makes it clear that we should fight against any form of divide between the secular and the sacred since we follow Christ 24/7. We are to make no distinction between the 'spiritual' parts of our lives (for example, reading the Bible or attending church) and the rest of our lives (i.e., family, work or education, rest and leisure). The danger is that we can compartmentalize our lives and fail to make the connection between our 'spiritual' activities and the other everyday things in our lives when, in fact, Christ is Lord over all of life.

God wants us to live seamlessly and not with two or more different identities according to the group of people we are with. Many postmoderns do this without even realizing it. The expression 'living *coram Deo*' (meaning 'in the presence of God') has even come into contemporary evangelical language to mean a sense of God's presence and a sense of wonder about life where God is never absent from anything we do. Unless we live out our relationship with God in everything, how can postmodern men and women understand the importance of faith in God as compared to seeing it as a 'lifestyle choice', which is a purely personal decision that only applies to our lives when we feel like it? That is why the time of wonder, stock-taking and getting to know God all contribute to knowing and living out our identity.

A loss of identity is perhaps one of the most tragic aspects of life in today's world. But as Christians, we do not have to create our identity. God gives it to us and that is how we learn to make sense of our life stories.[5] In other words, we learn how to fit our personal story into the biblical narrative (creation, the fall, the chosen people of the old covenant, redemption in Christ, the church in the world today and eternity) and to see how God has called and moulded us through the circumstances of life to be what we should be in his eyes at the present time and in our present circumstances.

Allow non-Christians to understand the gospel 'by walking in our landscape'

Paul makes it explicit in 1 Corinthians that non-Christians might attend the meetings of the gathered church: 'If an unbeliever or an inquirer [literally "someone without knowledge"] comes in' (1 Corinthians 14:24). At the weekly ordinary meetings of the church, they will see an extraordinary gathering of Christians, which has almost no equivalent in today's society. Men and women, people of all ages and social classes, people with different ethnic origins, people with totally different characters and temperaments all gathered to praise God, to learn more about him and to encourage each other.

I think that many people today have no idea what it means to be a Christian. They do not know that we can bring everything to the Lord in prayer. They do not realize all the practical and positive implications of being a disciple as we try to develop healthy relationships with each other. Welcoming people into the church community and into our worship is a powerful way to let people see what Christianity looks like in practice. Even so, you will probably have to work on several things in the church's public meetings:

- Welcome non-believers explicitly. Even if you are not sure whether there are any non-Christians present in a given week, saying

---

5 For further reflection on this question of identity, see Andrew Bunt, *Finding Your Best Identity* (London: IVP, 2022).

something such as, 'Whether you're already a long-term follower of Jesus or are coming to church for the very first time, we're delighted to have you here,' is welcoming and helps to set the expectation that believers can invite their non-Christian friends to the service.

- Avoid unnecessary religious jargon. If you are using useful technical terms (for example 'redemption'), then you must remember to give a brief explanation of the word.
- Explain clearly what is happening or what is going to happen. You can take nothing for granted and it is important to remember that people will not be in their 'comfort zone' when they attend a service for the first time.
- Connect the Bible's teaching with the congregation's daily lives and with the things that the media are talking about.
- Invite people to ask questions. In the sermon or in the leading of the service, you might say to people that if anything is strange or surprising to them, then the leaders or a Christian they came with would love to chat to them about it.

Putting it into practice

So, practically, what should happen when we meet together each Sunday? When we think of church revitalisation, what might a culturally adapted service look like?

A healthy church is a place where Christians can grow as disciples. Acts 2:42 lists several things that the early church did: they were devoted to the apostles' teaching, to fellowship, to the breaking of bread and to prayer. Does your church do all of this when you meet together on Sunday?

In general, our churches include a time of worship (with or without the breaking of bread, though Jesus remains central in both cases) and a time of Bible teaching. I think that this is true across a wide variety of churches. In some churches, the worship will be more structured, perhaps using a set liturgy and prayers, whereas others might be more spontaneous and give time for people to exercise their charismatic gifts. Whatever the style of worship and preaching, I believe that two other aspects should be included:

- practical teaching on discipleship in the widest sense
- prayer for each other as we go back out into the world

Is it legitimate to do this each Sunday? What does the New Testament teach about our 'services'? I think that there are two answers to this question. First, the New Testament makes it clear that worship is an attitude and not just a thing we do at a certain time of the week. Three verses define this kind of worship:

1 'Offer your bodies as a living sacrifice, holy and pleasing to God – this is your true and proper worship' (Romans 12:1).
2 'We who worship by the Spirit of God, who glory in Christ Jesus, and who put no confidence in the flesh' (Philippians 3:3).
3 'Let us be thankful, and so worship God acceptably with reverence and awe' (Hebrews 12:28).

The vocabulary used in the New Testament for the time when Christians gather is not 'service' (which is the literal translation of *latreia*, the Greek word for worship) but very ordinary words such as 'meeting' or 'when you come together'. You can see this in Acts 20:7–8; 1 Corinthians 11:17–18; 14:23–26; James 2:2 and in the poignant plea, 'Let us . . . not give up meeting together, as some are in the habit of doing, but encouraging one another' (Hebrews 10:24–25). Of course these meetings will include worship, whether it be formal or informal, but my fear is that as soon as an expression such as 'worship service' is used, Christians will have a preconceived idea of what is fitting for that occasion.

This understanding of the regular meeting of the church as a place to prepare us to live and love others as the scattered church opens up new possibilities. We are not limited to worship and to the teaching of Scripture. We gather to grow spiritually and to glorify God and that is why I think that we should find a way to include the aspects I mentioned at the beginning of this section, especially practical teaching on discipleship in the widest sense and prayer for each other as we go back out into the world.

Second, the Covid-19 pandemic revealed and accelerated certain trends in society. This forces us to deal with some of the practical issues facing Christians as we live out our lives as salt and light all through the week. Preparing to live 'in the world' also demands teaching that connects with the issues of the day. There is a danger that Christians live in a bubble in a vain attempt to be 'protected' from the influences of the world, but connecting the Bible to what people and the media are talking about, showing their relevance and giving Christians the words to express their faith in a way that makes sense are important ingredients of our weekly meetings both to build up Christians and to connect with non-Christians who may come to our services.

The need is real. A survey released in France showed that 85% of evangelical Christians wanted to receive such teaching in their churches, 'because they don't know what to say at their place of work as Christians when colleagues bring up topics concerning life and current issues'.[6]

What do I mean by practical issues? They will continue to emerge as society debates new topics, but here is a list of some of the themes that I taught in the church that I was pastoring when I wrote this chapter:

The postmodern world

- Secularism
- Fake news and conspiracy theories
- Facing up to Covid-19

Understanding history

- The church fathers, Augustine, Luther, Calvin and Blaise Pascal
- The history of missions

Culture

- TV, films, books, music and other media
- Where are people looking for meaning in our culture? Why do they watch soap operas and reality television? Is it a search for identity or for some sort of normality in a society that does not seem to offer any?
- What questions do we see being asked in the media or in best-selling books, and what are biblical answers?

Current issues

- Ecology
- Racism
- Violence
- Bioethics
- Sexual identity and ethics
- Poverty

---

6 The survey was organized by the CNEF in 2021. The full results (in French) can be found at www.lecnef.org/articles/86303-vivre-et-dire-l-evangile-au-travail-chiffres.

The wonders of creation

- The scientific method and its uses and abuses
- Great Christian scientists
- Neuroscience
- The miracle of language

Living as disciples

- Time management
- Money management
- Forgiveness
- Christians at work
- The use of social media
- Psychology
- Choice of leisure activities
- Addiction
- Marriage
- Family life

I am often asked how we can possibly do all of this when we meet together on a Sunday.[7] Each local church will have to think this out but, if we don't talk about these issues, where will Christians go to find the answers? They may surf the internet, but there's a lot of 'stuff' out there that may not be particularly helpful. Realistically, Sunday is the only time when nearly all the church members gather together, even if we organize special training days at other times.

A first line of response is the sermon, whether it is topical or expositional. Even with expositional preaching, it is possible to find a contemporary 'hook' around the difference that a Bible passage makes. This can be made clear in the sermon introduction so that listeners can know that it will have a pay-off in terms of relevance to their lives.

In today's world, depending on our local contexts and congregation, we could also make greater use of audiovisual aids (for example, films, documentaries and music videos). Much real 'philosophy' is done today through films and television series. The Reformation made the most of the printing press but today we learn more from internet tutorials, recorded lectures and so on. There is a risk that we become passive as we

---

7 You will find some more ideas on this subject in chapter 12.

use screens, so we must use them wisely by ensuring that there is 'local imprint' by enabling a time of sharing after an audiovisual sequence. This is a real bonus because these audiovisual productions do not often lead to such discussion and analysis in our daily lives.

This teaching helps to prepare Christians to live out their faith and to be witnesses for Christ all through the week as the scattered church but I feel that we can go further. Reading a good verse as a blessing at the end of the service is not enough. The congregation need real support as they face the upcoming week. A first step might be to help the church members to understand the context that others live in. This is why Neil Hudson of the London Institute for Contemporary Christianity suggests including a short interview each week on 'T. T. T.' ('This Time Tomorrow'), in which a church member talks about their work, their school or the way that they use their time in retirement.[8] In this way, people gain a better understanding of the issues that everyone is facing. This can be followed by a time of intercession (whatever form that takes) with some very specific prayer requests. Maybe someone has a job interview or an important doctor's appointment. Someone might want prayer for an elderly neighbour or a student might be taking an important exam. Perhaps another person has had a good chat about the gospel at work and is asking for wisdom for the next step in witnessing to a colleague. The needs and opportunities of the week are limitless.

In summary, the revitalisation team could think through how they can suggest some changes in the way that their church runs its Sunday services in order to include the four components of a weekly church meeting that we have seen in this chapter. To communicate this to the church as a whole, the following acronym may prove useful: what are our AIMS when we meet together?

- Adoration: worship in amazement at God's grace towards us
- Issues: training disciples to live in today's world
- Mission: sending out the congregation as the scattered church
- Scriptures: biblical teaching

---

8 To read more about how church services can include this dimension, I recommend Neil Hudson, *Scattered and Gathered: Equipping Disciples for the Frontline* (London: IVP, 2019).

Where do we go from here?

Maybe some of these ideas on spirituality are too radical for your church to go there straight away but, whatever your situation, the revitalisation team must think about how to apply the principle of helping the congregation to live a truly spiritual life and how the gathered church can be God's instrument for this, which is God's intention. How can we change things so that the congregation will marvel at who God is and what he has done and is doing? How can we ensure that we do this with reverence and creativity? How can we make it relevant for today's world?

A lot of ideas have been proposed in this chapter. The next one will concentrate on some practical ways in which the leadership team can work on revitalising the church in the three main areas we have been discussing. We will look at this through the lens of discipleship.

12
Discipleship in a healthy church

Discipleship means being a learner. A church that is undergoing re-vitalisation will have to think through the implications that its vision and strategy will have on discipleship. Above all, and quite simply, discipleship is learning to live with God and for his glory.

There is no reason for Christians to be on the defensive. We have the best message in the world and being a Christian is by far the best way of life we can possibly imagine. But we need to hear this 'better story'.[1] Rather than trying to protect ourselves from the world, we must listen to a better song.

Two stories from Greek mythology can help us to understand this. They both recount an incident involving sirens (mythical creatures that have developed to become our mermaids). Their beautiful songs attract sailors who approach the rocks where the sirens are, only to be shipwrecked. The expression 'to listen to the siren song' is still used in French to refer to the danger of listening to or being tempted by attractive but misleading or even perilous speech.

The first story is taken from *The Odyssey*. Odysseus and his companions are returning from the Land of the Dead. As they approach the sirens' rocks, Odysseus remembers the words of Circe:

> Be careful, if you listen to the songs of the sirens, they will attract you and you and the sailors will die. You must prepare balls of wax to put in the ears of your companions to prevent them from hearing the sirens. You yourself will be allowed to listen to them

---

1 This is an allusion to the title of the book by Glynn Harrison, *A Better Story: God, Sex and Human Flourishing* (London: IVP, 2017). It is an excellent example of the principle of being positive about our Christian convictions. I first heard the illustration from Greek mythology used in this chapter in a lecture given by Glynn Harrison at the European Leadership Forum.

but on one condition: you must be attached to the mast of your boat and, when you beg your companions to detach you, they must not listen.[2]

Odysseus prepares the balls of wax and gives them to his companions, then the crew ties him to the mast of the boat. When they approach the sirens, Odysseus hears their melancholy songs and begs his companions to release him, which of course they refuse to do.

The second story is about Orpheus and the ship *The Argo*. Returning from Colchis, the Argonauts pass the sirens' rocks but Orpheus stands on the deck of the boat. Unlike Odysseus, he is not tied down. The sound of his lyre and his beautiful singing cover the song of the sirens and the Argonauts are able to pass by quietly and escape the sirens' dangerous songs.

What can these stories show us, as Christians? Trying to block out the sirens' call by being bound to legalism or attempting to avoid listening to 'the world' is less likely to be effective than being thrilled by who God is and by our new identity in Christ. With this in mind, what practical steps should we include in our revitalisation strategy?

It is in the gathered church that we learn to love God and other people. The word 'disciple' means learner and the key to revitalising the church is that the individuals within it should be learners too. I do not believe that we see a group of especially committed Christians called disciples in the New Testament. In fact, we are all disciples: 'The *disciples* were called Christians first at Antioch' (Acts 11:26, my emphasis). In addition, everything we do as churches is 'discipling'. It is not some elaborate programme that a Christian goes through, even if it may involve one-to-one or small-group sharing at times. People can be helped to become disciples through preaching, Bible study, prayer meetings, the example of mature Christians, sharing and special training sessions. Everything adds up to enabling Christians to grow in their faith.

In this chapter, I have divided this learning process into the three dimensions that we have already been examining (social, societal and spiritual). In each case, I have first summarized the content that is mentioned in the revitalisation flow chart (see chapter 5).

---

2 This summary of Circe's speech is my own. See *The Odyssey*, XII for the full story.

The social dimension

Discipleship in order to live well as the scattered church sent by Jesus into the world to build relationships, to do good and to share the gospel in four relational networks: family, workplace or education, community, and leisure time or friends

The church needs to hear from the Bible that we all (without exception) have been sent to go and love others. This will include explaining the gospel at the right time and place. I produced a film for the CNEF that was shown in churches to help Christians to understand this.[3] The title (*Envoyés*) means sent, which is based on the verse: 'as the Father has sent me, I am sending you' (John 20:21). After greeting his disciples, these were the first words that Jesus spoke to them after his resurrection.

Living this out in the world needs teaching on family life (including how to live a healthy relationship as a couple or bring up children well) and work (including motivation and relationships and not just witnessing at the coffee machine). Teaching is also needed on leisure activities and healthy friendships. I wrote a book about this for the Groupes Bibliques Universitaires (GBU, a French student movement) because I could not find an existing book that was biblically positive about leisure activities without falling into the twin traps of lack of priorities and legalism.[4] Friendship includes both face-to-face, real-life relationships and the use of social media (and a lot more could be written on how we can make the most of that opportunity to share our lives as Christians). Teaching is necessary in all of these areas, but hard thinking, sharing and discussion among Christians must also be part of the process.

The same goes for our commitment to our community in the area in which we live. Do we have non-Christian friends? How can we encourage each other to exercise hospitality? Should we become involved in social or humanitarian work, either as a church-based activity or in a secular organization?

We have to convince every Christian that the best means of evangelism is their own daily life. Churches often feel the need to organize an

---

3 REMEEF, FMEF, CNEF, RES, Mouvement de Lausanne, *Envoyés*, 2018. You can find the film (with English subtitles) at www.envoyes-lefilm.com.
4 David Brown, *Mes loisirs, comment choisir?* (Paris: Farel/PBU, 2017).

evangelistic campaign to 'mobilize the troops' but, compared to the proven way of spreading the gospel (i.e., through relationships), I have the impression that these campaigns are not very effective in today's world, except where they encourage Christians to bring along to meetings friends and acquaintances with whom they have already built a relationship. That said, Christians also need instruction, mentoring and prayer to avoid the dangers of becoming conformed to the pattern of this world (see Romans 12:2). We are in the world but not of the world and we need to be saturated by the word in order to be faithful (see John 17:16–19). That is also part of discipleship.

So far, I have not mentioned children and young people in this book, mainly because my conception of the way that a healthy church should function should include them naturally (while accepting that they may still be on the path to a personal faith). But I must add that this paragraph is particularly true for these age groups. Children and young people in the church need good biblical answers to the questions that their teachers and classmates will bring up and encouragement to see that the Christian way makes good sense and that there is no need to feel ashamed to be part of a church family. As we saw earlier in the book, one of the factors that is leading to decline in the church may well be that the next generation has not been entrusted with leadership and that the baton has not been passed on. For that to happen, each generation must keep the same passion for the faith as the generations that came before it. Routine, boring services and an absence of wonder will not do that. Living out the truth is the key.

A good way to help disciples put the social dimension into practice is to communicate that Christian life can be a daily adventure. Every day, we can ask God to put people on our path – people we can care for and love and with whom we can share the good news – and ask him to help us to recognize them when they appear. In a world where so many people are suffering, we have countless opportunities to help where help is desperately needed. This can lead to opportunities to explain that we have learned this happy way of life from Jesus who has done so much for us.

The societal dimension

Discipleship in order to have a relevant witness
Understanding today's society and helping Christians to speak to the issues

The Bible teaching in a church must be applied to today's society. This may be a challenge to the pastor and the teaching team but, if Christians cannot be taught in their church to understand the relevance of the Bible in today's world, where else can they go? Of course there is the internet but, since not everything you can find online is biblical or healthy, it is the responsibility of the pastor to suggest good-quality websites and to help the congregation to develop discernment. Another possibility is to invite a guest speaker to help Christians to understand the issues. Yet another is to use the resources within the church. For example, you may be able to bring church members who have skills, knowledge and experience in healthcare into dialogue with the pastoral team with their knowledge of Scripture and theology.

The exhortation in Colossians that I have already quoted regarding the social dimension of our discipleship is also apposite here: 'Let your conversation be always full of grace, seasoned with salt, so that you may know how to answer everyone' (Colossians 4:6). To have a solid Christian point of view is one thing but to communicate it to our fellow citizens is another. I remember preaching in my church about same-sex marriage. Two-thirds of my sermon was about suggesting ways to express what the Bible says on the subject so that, in the course of a conversation with a non-Christian, biblical ethics would not be rejected as something from a past age but understood as a coherent, plausible approach from our biblical presuppositions. We do not hate people for being different, we are just offering a better way.

The spiritual dimension

Discipleship in order to build a relationship with God
Learning to trust and obey God 24/7
Increasing knowledge of Scripture by teaching and dialogue
Adults learn by talking to each other

A few years ago, I wrote a small book on discipleship. In order to clarify my thinking on the biblical teaching, I went on a personal mini-retreat at my son's house in Brittany in the west of France. There, I read the whole of the New Testament (it only took a couple of days) and noted down every instruction that was given to us as disciples. Although the word is not used in the Epistles, I took the teaching in them to be for Christians as disciples.

I found that practically everything could be included under just four main themes:

1 worshipping God (loving God)
2 trusting God
3 obeying God (fighting the good fight)
4 loving others (doing good to the people that God brings into my life)

These fundamentals contribute to the overall daily life of believers as they become more and more satisfied in Christ and further convinced that there is no better way to live. As Christians work towards applying these four objectives, we discover that they help us to live seamlessly between church life and our daily life in the world. In fact, the word 'today' figures frequently in the exhortations to worship, trust and obey.

We have already looked at length at the fourth aspect, loving others, in chapters 7 and 8, so let's turn to the other three themes.

Worshipping God

After recovering from his illness, King Hezekiah exclaimed, 'The living, the living – they praise you, as I am doing today' (Isaiah 38:19). Several centuries later, Jesus told the Samaritan woman that the time was coming when true worshippers would worship in spirit and in truth. That time came on the day of Pentecost, when the church came into being, and it is still the case today. We do not need to go to a special place to worship God. We can adore him as we walk down the street, as we wait at the bus stop or as we prepare a meal, giving thanks to God all through the day and remembering his gracious love towards us.

Discipleship includes learning to do this but worship is also a collective activity and discipleship must bear in mind the different temperaments we have and how this affects the way that we approach God. In his book, *Sacred Pathways*,[5] Gary Thomas identifies nine different outlooks on life that can influence our relationship with God. It may be necessary for a local church to offer a diversity of services within the same fellowship in order to help some of these specific categories of people:

---

5 Gary Thomas, *Sacred Pathways: Nine Ways to Connect with God* (Grand Rapids, MI: Zondervan, 2010).

1 Naturalists who love God out of doors because nature proclaims how great God is.
2 Sensates who love God with their senses and enjoy services in which they are drawn to see his majesty.
3 Traditionalists who love God through ritual and symbol.
4 Ascetics who love God in solitude, silence and simplicity.
5 Activists who love God through confrontation and think of church as a place to recharge their batteries so that they can go back into the world to wage war against injustice.
6 Caregivers who love God by loving and serving others.
7 Enthusiasts who love God and are not satisfied with simply knowing concepts but also want to experience them and be moved by them.
8 Contemplatives who love God through spending time in adoration in order to love God more completely.
9 Intellectuals who love God with their minds and always desire to study doctrines, issues or concepts.

Trusting God

A large part of our Christian walk is learning to depend on God in all circumstances. 'So that your trust may be in the LORD, I teach you *today*, even you' (Proverbs 22:19, my emphasis). 'Give us *today* our daily bread' (Matthew 6:11, my emphasis). Bread is a concrete example but trust is a characteristic attitude of the disciples of Jesus in every area of our lives.

Many of the Psalms dwell on trust in God when everything seems hopeless and the New Testament teaching on prayer repeatedly returns to the fact that Christians need not be anxious about anything but, as Paul writes, 'in every situation, by prayer and petition, with thanksgiving, present your requests to God. And the peace of God, which transcends all understanding, will guard your hearts and your minds in Christ Jesus' (Philippians 4:6–7). Within the church, we need to encourage each other to trust God. We have real hope, whatever happens, and this will undoubtedly be seen by those around us who have no such confidence by which to live their lives.

Obeying God

This good fight covers many areas of our lives: developing a Christian character; daring to be known as Christians by the people around us;

praying; bringing up our children; remaining sexually pure; thinking through our faith in our profession and working for the good of others. 'But encourage one another daily, as long as it is called *today*, so that none of you may be hardened by sin's deceitfulness' (Hebrews 3:13, my emphasis). The model of Alcoholics Anonymous (AA) is very useful here. Members of AA never promise that they will never drink alcohol again. Their challenge is to abstain today because those twenty-four hours are the only ones when they can act. Yesterday is gone and tomorrow never comes but they can decide not to drink today. The same principle applies to Christians in their daily fight to please God and to resist temptation.

We often prefer to wallow in nostalgia ('Things were better in the past.') or to live in a hypothetical future ('Everything will be fine when I pass my exams, or find a job, or get married, or buy a nice house or retire.') but it is heroic to live in the present. Every disciple has to trust and obey in their particular context and with their particular temperament in order to walk with Jesus *today*. The revitalisation team needs to think this through as they plan their strategy because the health of the church depends on the growth of every disciple. To effectively help disciples to grow, it might be necessary to organize several different types of service (known as targeted services) according to the make-up of the congregation. As we have already mentioned, home groups or one-to-one mentoring are also useful ways to contribute to disciple-making.

Different challenges should be dealt with explicitly when we meet together as Christians. We must also remember that different age groups are faced with different problems. For many people, life involves moving through different stages and facing different challenges in each period. When we are young, we are concerned with finding out who we are and discovering our particular identity. From the age of about thirty, our big questions concern our purpose in life from the point we have reached, whether that is focused on our job, our family or our other relationships. These can be such a struggle that we have little time to think about anything else, including our Christian commitment. In mid-life, pressures of time and responsibility weigh heavily on us (for example, teenage children, aging parents or promotions at work). Those who are single can also face the additional challenge of not fitting in with what a church often treats as the typical pattern of family life. Then, as retirement approaches, there are doubts about what we have accomplished, fears about our health and sometimes worries about our adult children. Finally, old age means facing up to the reality of death and the realization that few people are aware of who we were and what we did for the Lord in our youth.

Ultimately, this should take us back to Scripture. While our spirituality will have many different expressions, the controlling foundation must be Bible-based. In concluding this chapter, I want to insist on the knowledge of the Bible as the very basis of our spirituality as evangelical Christians. Not tradition. Not the words of the latest praise song. Not a selection of our favourite verses. As we face up to the challenges and to the complexity of life today, we need to dig into the Bible to see what it is saying and learn how to apply it.

What does this mean in practice?

I have been writing about *what* discipleship should be and not *how* it should happen. There are all sorts of ideas about the most effective methods of discipleship. They will depend on your local situation and the availability of disciple-makers. Christians learn in the *context* of the gathered church with people they know and love. But the *content* of discipleship is what matters in order for Christians to live their lives as part of the scattered church.

Here are a few practical ideas which might be useful in your situation:

- Provide systematic teaching of the word, seeing the big picture and the storyline of human history from God's perspective. This will model good hermeneutics to the congregation.
- Read the Bible in church services in a dynamic way or use dramatized readings with several voices.
- Encourage church members to read through whole sections of the Bible. In our church, we have occasional reading projects when all the members read through a whole book of the Bible at the same speed, day by day, during a whole month.
- Start conversations among church members ('Adults learn by talking to each other,' as it says in the revitalisation flow chart). Talking together about a Bible passage can help people to understand and apply what they have read.
- Pray earnestly that we can live out what we learn and share our prayer needs with Christians in our social networks or in messaging apps.

Much more could be said. My prayer is that God would grant discernment, wisdom and creativity to each revitalisation team reading this book. In the next chapter, we will see how to set the process in motion after this important preparation period.

A small town near Manchester, UK

In the months after the first meeting in Martin and Carol's home, the church had come a long way. Thanks to the survey that the congregation had completed, the group set up to pilot the revitalisation process had a clear view of the true state of the church and the aspirations of the members. They had come up with a number of strategic proposals that they wished to communicate to the church. The challenge now was to help the church to accept these ideas wholeheartedly. The elders realized that they were dealing with spiritual issues and not just a list of good ideas.

This Sunday morning, Trevor Chapman was the preacher. He had been asked to outline the spiritual basis of the project that they had been working on.

Tom and Jane settled into their seats and found the passage that Trevor had asked them to turn to in their Bibles: the beginning of 1 Corinthians. Tom still liked to use his nice hardback edition of the Bible, but Jane preferred to read the text on her smartphone, which she could easily slip into her handbag.

Trevor started by reading a couple of verses. 'In chapter 1, verses 22 and 23, we see that the Jews demand miraculous signs and the Greeks look for wisdom, but, says Paul, we preach Christ crucified. In many ways, these attitudes are still with us today. But the gospel hasn't changed. The cross and resurrection of Jesus are still absolutely central. We see in verse 24 that Christ is the power of God and the wisdom of God.'

At this point, Trevor asked one of the church members, Mrs Connolly, to come and read the whole of 1 Corinthians 2. She had been asked to do the Bible reading on several Sunday mornings now. Her voice was so pleasant, her diction was so clear and the intonation of her voice so meaningful that the words came alive. Tom realized that he didn't know this chapter as well as chapter 1.

Trevor continued. 'Paul was very aware of his weakness and counted on God's intervention, just concentrating on Jesus Christ and him crucified. And yet he can still write, in verse 6, that "we do, however, speak a message of wisdom" though that's not a wisdom understood by the leaders of this world. Indeed, as verses 9 to 12 explain, only those who are born again of the Spirit can know this wisdom.'

Tom nodded in agreement. There didn't seem much wisdom around today with all the fake news and conspiracy theories online and on social networks.

Trevor seemed to have read his mind. 'T. S. Eliot wrote about how we're in danger of losing wisdom in knowledge,' he said.

Trevor taught English literature in a local school and loved to refer to books other than the Bible. 'If Paul can do it in Athens, I don't see why I cannot do it here in our town,' he liked to quip.

Trevor went on. 'We need this wisdom, brothers and sisters. The end of the chapter gives us two remarkable ways of understanding it. In verse 12, it's when we understand "what God has freely given us". It's in understanding the gospel, living by the gospel, seeing all the consequences and implications of the gospel. Then in verse 16, it's having "the mind of Christ". In other words, thinking like Christ and seeing things like Christ.'

Tom wondered what conclusion Trevor was going to draw from that and how it would help the revitalisation process but he was impressed by the closing remarks.

'So how does Jesus see his church and how should we see it?' Trevor asked. 'He knows and understands what's at stake in the cosmic battle between God and evil. He knows the real challenge of living on this earth in light of this conflict. And so what does he want for his people? Two things, I think. We have to ask ourselves how we can best prepare ourselves to love God and to live for his glory in today's world and how we can reach out to non-Christians at this time in history, communicating how much they need salvation and the gospel. May the Lord help us do this. Amen.'

Tom said, 'Yes, that's it! Well done, Trevor. Amen indeed. Those are the two basic issues we should never forget. That's why we want to move out of routine in the church and live for Jesus in our town!'

Jane switched off her phone and smiled contentedly. She and Tom had taken the right decision to stick with the church.

A city in the west of France

Denis had attended the new evening service initiated by Guillaume and Valérie twice and he had to admit that it was extremely refreshing. He loved the times of quiet meditation and he had learnt a lot (yes, even as a full-time pastor!) from the social issues they had raised during those meetings.

All of this was on his mind as he drove his car out of the city and up into the hills for his monthly prayer day. He had started doing this as a young pastor and it had become a regular fixture in his calendar. The time set aside to think and pray away from the bustle of the city had often helped him to see the direction of his ministry more clearly and had enabled him to find answers to various problems that had arisen over the years.

This morning, he had the impression that he was at a crossroads like never before. The leadership team were beginning to realize that the church was stuck in a rut. Some of the younger couples were showing the way forward but he was painfully aware that his seminary training hadn't prepared him to lead this change. The previous week, he had attended a two-day seminar organized by his denomination on church revitalisation – a new concept for him. He had noted down several ideas and he wanted to spend the day thinking them through before God.

When he arrived at his favourite spot, he decided to read the whole of the book of Nehemiah, which had been at the core of the seminar. Then he munched the apple that his wife had put in his bag and tried to pray about the two main issues that the speaker at the seminar had identified.

The first question involved the discipleship of Christians: how can we help Christians to love God and to love others with the particular challenges of this time in history? As Denis prayed, he saw only too clearly that all sorts of traditions and practices had grown up over the thirty years since the church had been planted. Not bad things, but he wondered how much they were based in Scripture. He had always tried to follow current affairs so he knew that Christians were under pressure to accept other lifestyles, especially as this was being aggressively promoted by the media. Was their church truly helping Christians to grow in their faith today?

After a meagre lunch, he used the afternoon to pray about the second question: how can we reach out to the people around us, communicating the gospel in ways that they can understand? As he prayed for all the Christians on the church membership list, the reality jumped off the page: very few had been converted in recent times and even fewer from a totally non-Christian background.

Denis found himself watching an ant crawl across the log he was sitting on. Did it know where it was going? What instinct was guiding it along with the other ants from its nest? It was like an object lesson for Denis. He prayed that the Lord would give him more imagination to see how the church could do things differently, to see something which didn't yet exist.

He couldn't deny that he was frightened. What would the church members think? Could he even lose his job? And what if revitalisation divided the church? And then there was the fear of failure. What if the changes didn't work? Wouldn't it be better to play it safe and stay in his comfort zone? But then he remembered one of his favourite verses, a promise that he had held on to from the days at university when he was afraid that he hadn't done enough revision for a particular exam: 'Cast all your anxiety on him because he cares for you' (1 Peter 5:7).

'Yes,' he thought, as he drove back home. 'I've come a long way in the past couple of months but the adventure is just starting. There's no turning back now. The Lord's glory is at stake in our city.'

A village in central Romania

As planned, the whole of this Sunday morning had been devoted to communicating the idea of the scattered church without saying the words. Sunday came and went. No one got upset. No one wrote a letter to resign from the church. Stefan had grown up in a communist country and in his head he could hear the words, 'The revolution is underway.' This time, the revolution was a spiritual one.

He still had a lot of questions. What was the best way forward? He half remembered a joke from the soviet era:

We went to work but we didn't work.
We didn't work but we accomplished the five-year plan.
We accomplished the five-year plan but there was nothing
    in the shops.
There was nothing in the shops but we had things at home.
We had things at home but we weren't happy.
We weren't happy but we re-elected the same government.

He knew that the revitalisation group needed to draw up an ongoing strategy, but he also knew how sceptical people were about 'five-year plans'. As it was, several of his church members only had enough income to feed their family week by week. There was no way that they could think long-term. It takes time to change long-ingrained habits in any organization, and things needed to happen to encourage change. The ELF mentoring group leaders had said people needed to see 'short-term gains'. But what could they be in their context?

The following Thursday afternoon, his thoughts were interrupted by the phone ringing. It was the church caretaker calling. 'Stefan, come quickly. There's a big problem at the church. The place is flooded!'

Stefan put on his jacket and ran to the building, which was only 300 metres away. When he opened the main door, he couldn't believe his eyes. There was a major leak in the heating system and the water was two centimetres deep all over the floor.

Stefan tried to think quickly. His first thought was what the long-term damage might be. This was quickly replaced by a more pressing need: what would they do this Sunday? There was no way that the congregation could meet here.

Then he remembered Grigore's words: 'People, not programmes.'

'Maybe this is our opportunity,' Stefan said. 'It's like God's sense of humour to make us do things in a different way. We'll have to decentralize our gathering this weekend and meet in each other's homes.' His mind was racing now. 'That means I'll have to make an outline for a Bible study and maybe I could record a sermon and put it online and make a list of prayer requests. I need to contact the elders and a few other people to lead the groups. Then I'll have to get families to agree to welcome groups into their homes and let everyone know where to go.'

With the help of Ana and Grigore, he managed to do all of this in the space of forty-eight hours. By Sunday afternoon, he was exhausted but, by the middle of the week, he had received so much positive feedback that his exhaustion changed to elation.

At their next meeting, the church elders decided to make this a monthly event, and Stefan was wondering if the repairs to the church building couldn't make it a more attractive place to invite people to. And all because of a leak in the heating system.

Stefan's thoughts turned to the prophet Isaiah: 'For my thoughts are not your thoughts, neither are your ways my ways' (Isaiah 55:8).

'That's true, even in church revitalisation,' he mused.

IMPLEMENTING THE VISION

13
Starting the movement

The last six chapters on the three dimensions of revitalisation have been heavy. You may be thinking, 'Wow. How can we incorporate all that into our plans to revitalise our church?' The good news is that you don't have to. The important thing is to have a feel for what God is calling us to do as his people in order to glorify his name at the present time.

No church can change radically in a short space of time. The good news also comes with a warning: this stage of drawing up a strategic plan for your church is indispensable. The overall vision must be fleshed out with practical steps to give it concrete reality in the church. We need to pray and plan, seek 'the mind of Christ', that is, 'wisdom among the mature', as compared to the, 'wisdom of this age or of the rulers of this age' (1 Corinthians 2:16, 6). Then, we must put this wisdom into practice by drawing up good plans that are right for our local situation.

As we have already seen, the revitalisation team must make a courageous analysis of the state of the church and reach an agreement on the initial strategy to propose to the church. This is not just an intellectual exercise but a process that should be carried out in prayer and humility. Paul wrote to the Philippians:

> And this is my prayer: that your love may abound more and more in knowledge and depth of insight, so that you may be able to discern what is best and may be pure and blameless for the day of Christ, filled with the fruit of righteousness that comes through Jesus Christ – to the glory and praise of God.
> (Philippians 1:9–11)

I am assuming at this point that, based on the vision of a healthy church, you have drawn up an action plan (you may wish to look at the final paragraphs of chapter 6 to check that you have got to this point). Below, you will see an example of an action plan for the first year of change. I must insist that this is only an example of the sort of thing that your team might come up with. The objective is to take the first achievable steps towards the vision.

Some people might be surprised that I have not written anything about the financial aspects of revitalisation. The reason is simple: most of the things that we have talked about in this book are not expensive. The only exception would be if your church building needs a lot of repairs or modernization. The fundamental changes concern our beliefs, convictions and attitudes and do not involve huge sums of money, though they may be harder to change.

Strategy for change: action plan for year 1

To help to introduce the process, invite a pastor from a church that has gone through a successful revitalisation to preach at the Sunday service and to give a talk about what happened in their church.

The social dimension

- Redecorate and reorganize the church entrance area and offer coffee before the morning service to enable more contact between members. Include this in the church budget.
- Set up a church group in a messaging app or online group so that the church community can keep in touch during the week. Encourage people to use it to connect and support one another spiritually, socially and practically.
- Teach on the biblical basis for hospitality and encourage church members to invite their neighbours to their homes (for example, for a meal, barbecue or drinks).
- Teach church members and the young people how to bring the gospel into their relationships in an authentic and natural way.

The societal dimension

- Organize a Saturday morning 'seminar' for the church members to help them to understand today's society. Invite a speaker from a denominational theological seminary, an apologetics-based mission agency or parachurch ministry to give a talk and to lead a discussion on the ways that the church can adapt to its cultural context.

- Ask a group of young people to redesign the church website to make it welcoming, accessible and understandable to non-Christians in your local community.

The spiritual dimension

- Set up prayer triplets within the church where people can meet every week to pray for each other and for the friends and neighbours whom they want to reach with the gospel.
- Preach an expository sermon series on the letter to the Romans to help every church member to understand and be in wonder of the gospel of our Lord Jesus Christ.
- Show the film *Paul, Apostle of Christ*[1] followed by discussion groups to share what people saw and how this could be applied to their lives.
- Start an alternative, more meditative Sunday evening service as an experiment for six months.

Starting the movement

After this important preparation period, we come to the next section of the revitalisation flow chart shown at the end of chapter 5. The chart specifies four aspects of the launch of the revitalisation process:

1 communicate so that people understand and adhere to the vision and the strategy for change
2 involve as many people as possible
3 produce short-term gains
4 persevere

Communicate

Communication allows people to understand and adhere to the vision and the strategy for change. This can be done in a variety of ways. For example, a written document can be distributed at a church meeting during which the main elements of the vision and the process are explained, preferably with visual elements such as photos, diagrams and graphics to help engage with people. Projecting a presentation for people to follow can be helpful

---

1 Andrew Hyatt, *Paul, Apostle of Christ*, 2018.

if you can use it effectively and keep each slide simple and focused. It can sometimes be helpful to invite someone from another church to tell the story of how revitalisation was beneficial.

In some circumstances, the revitalisation team may need to present the vision and strategy in stages, convincing first the pastoral team (the pastor and elders), then the church board and finally the whole church. The key to communication is to repeat, repeat, repeat. Although it is not necessary to give the whole vision and action plan every time, the team should use every opportunity to remind people of where the church is going and why.

Above all, we need to communicate the fundamental reasons for change. When my children were small, they used to mock me by calling me 'Daddy-because' because (!) I always tried to give them the reasons for my instructions.

There will no doubt be a certain number of Christians who do not like change (very few people do). We have to convey that what we are doing can help them to grow in their Christian lives and we have to communicate the logic of the proposed changes that flow from the vision. In other words, we need to describe it in such a way that others can begin to see what the future will be like and want to be part of it.

Involve as many people as possible

It is vital to involve as many people as possible because revitalisation will never happen if the church members see it as a top-down process being imposed on them from above. While the leadership team will try to ensure an overall direction and vision, it is crucial to encourage people to think creatively about the ways that they can all work towards the vision. That is why I have mentioned the concept of a learning community in several places in this book.

As we enter the stage called 'starting the movement' on the flow chart, it would be wise to ask the whole body of believers to validate the vision of a healthy church. You can find a printable diagram at https://www.revitalisation.fr/en/strategy. A church meeting can approve the vision and commit to praying for it to become a reality, praying for the leadership team, for unity in the tough decisions and for God to be glorified both by the changes and by the way in which they are experienced by church members. A special Sunday service could be devoted to launching the vision officially, as members covenant together to go through the process with love, humility and patience.

Then, as plans begin to be implemented, as many people as possible should be involved as active partners. Delegation is the key.

Produce short-term gains

The process of revitalisation can gain traction if people see that it has made an immediate positive impact. I have a colleague who calls this 'picking the low-hanging fruit'. It could be something very down to earth such as making the church building easier to use and thus less embarrassing to invite friends to come to, for instance by improving the lighting in the main room or by renovating the toilet area.

Persevere

Before becoming a pastor, I taught English as a foreign language and I remember the words in the preface of one of the textbooks I used: 'The world is full of people who have started to learn English.' The danger lies in becoming satisfied too soon with what has been started when the revitalisation project is only halfway to fulfilment.

All of these aspects are leadership skills, so this is an appropriate moment to look at what leadership means both in general and in the context of revitalisation. This will be the subject of the next chapter before we move into the final part of this book: working towards lasting change.

A small town near Manchester, UK

Tom was devastated. He hadn't believed his ears when Jane had told him at breakfast. Were they really going to close down the big department store on the high street? Of course he knew the economic reasons for out-of-town shopping. People preferred to go by car to the supermarket. It was easy to park and there were all sorts of restaurants and other stores in the vicinity. But he felt such a sense of loss.

Tom had grown up in the town and that store had been a magical place. When he was a little boy, he had gone there to buy sweets with his pocket money. At Christmas, the whole family had bought presents there and he had visited Father Christmas' grotto. As a teenager, he had gone to the milkshake bar with his friends, hoping to meet girls. As a young man, he and Jane had bought their first kitchen equipment and curtains there. He still dropped in to get odds and ends such as batteries or bulbs for the garden. There were so many memories stretching all through his life. What was 'progress' worth if it meant the disappearance of the things that he had grown up with and loved?

But then it dawned on him: this was exactly what some of the old faithful members of the church were feeling about the revitalisation project. They had grown up in the church. They loved the old dark wood fittings that the younger members found depressing, they enjoyed the old hymns that they knew by heart and they felt reassured by the routine of the services. As the younger members would say, it was all part of their 'comfort zone'.

As Tom thought about it, he came to the conclusion that he should spend more time with these people. He should listen to their memories and let them know that he understood by telling them his reaction to the closure of the department store. He could explain how he had come to terms with it. He could help them to understand that we live in a world that is continually changing, often for the better. He was sure that most of them preferred the comforts of their homes now to the rather dark and dismal houses that many of them had known in their youth. In any case, in the face of change, Christians are privileged people because we trust in Jesus who is the same yesterday, today and forever.

Tom shared all of this with Jane when they sat down together for their evening meal. Jane was less nostalgic than Tom but she understood what he was saying and agreed that it was something that they could do together. As always, Jane's practical nature took over and, no sooner said than done, she had phoned one of the elderly couples from the church and arranged to go for coffee with them the following Saturday morning.

A city in the west of France

It came out of the blue. Guillaume and Valérie were astounded. It was late one Sunday evening when Guillaume found a new email in his inbox. Not the best time of the week to discover a message like this:

Dear Guillaume and Valérie,
You are destroying our church.

Before you started making all your suggestions to pastor Denis, there was a good atmosphere here. We enjoyed getting together on a Sunday morning. The worship was brilliant. The teaching was good.

But this morning, Denis preached on money. I'm up to my ears dealing with finance all week. I don't come to church to hear more on that subject.

People are getting upset.

You have a lot to answer for.
Marcel

Guillaume and Valérie knew who Marcel was: a man in his mid-thirties, an insurance agent by trade, married to Sylvie, a primary school teacher, with two young children. He was usually quite reserved but, once or twice, he had come close to losing his temper at church business meetings. Afterwards, people had said that he was suffering from lack of sleep with two young children at home or maybe from the pressure of his job. This time, it seemed different. Needless to say, Guillaume and Valérie didn't get much sleep that night either.

At breakfast the next morning, they decided that Guillaume should write a short response and they agreed on a conciliatory form of words:

Dear Marcel,
We are so sorry to hear that you are worried about changes at the church.

Could we meet up for a drink after work tonight and have a chat about these concerns?
Guillaume

Fortunately, Marcel agreed. At six o'clock, they met in a café in the city centre, which happened to be quite close to where they both worked. Drinking a beer together can do wonders to calm down conflicts.

Marcel tried to explain what he meant. 'All week long I hear my clients complaining about everything under the sun. And the news on television is always so depressing. Either something bad has just happened or it's going to happen soon, according to the 'experts'. I just want an hour on Sunday morning when I can forget all that and praise God with all my heart.'

'I understand. I need that too,' Guillaume said. 'But I must admit that I sometimes find it all a bit repetitive. I need more stimulation. I need to see how it all connects with my daily life. But tell me, honestly, are there a lot of people who're upset about the changes that are happening in our church?'

Marcel hesitated, sipped his beer, and then admitted that it was a bit of an exaggeration. 'Maybe one or two people have reservations. But, if I'm honest, that's probably because they don't like any change at all. As far as I'm concerned, life can be a burden far too often. Our little Samuel only seems to sleep for about six hours a night, and Sylvie and I could do with a couple of weeks of holiday where we could get a good rest. But even then, the children would be with us. We don't have family nearby who could take them for a few days.'

Guillaume felt sorry for Marcel. He realized that we don't always know why people react the way they do. Refusing to think about social issues wasn't a solution and he wanted to get back to that question but first, he needed to offer some practical help.

'Listen, Marcel. I know Valérie and I don't have a lot of experience with children, but we could have them on a Saturday afternoon from time to time to give you a breather. What do you think?'

Marcel was touched by the offer. 'I'll talk it over with Sylvie,' he said.

Guillaume wasn't finished. 'As I see it, the people around us are facing the same problems we are. Bringing up the children, stress at work, money and also more existential questions like the climate or talking to their children about gender issues. That's why we have to dig into these questions as Christians to see how our faith in Jesus makes a difference. It's good for us and it helps us to connect with others. They want to see how Christians deal with these things. That's what'll make our witness more plausible.'

Marcel drank the last drops from his glass. 'Thanks for the chat, Guillaume. We should do this more often. It's good to be able to open your heart to someone. It makes me grateful to be part of our church family.'

A village in central Romania

A few months later, everyone could feel a difference in the church. People knew each other better thanks to the home groups once a month on Sunday mornings and Stefan's preaching had helped the congregation to understand some of the issues in today's world. Sometimes it took a lot of time and effort but he was encouraged by the response of the congregation and he was delighted that the Christians were trying to reach out to people around them. Gone were the days when the church members thought that sanctification meant separation from non-Christians through fear of being 'contaminated by the world'.

Three new members had been integrated into the initial revitalisation group and, best of all, the team had been officially recognized by the church members as a valid part of the church structure.

However, one question kept rearing its head. Stefan explained this to Ana as they were driving to the next town to visit her uncle. 'Several of the younger people have been telling me that, if we truly want to grow, we should copy what they're doing over in that new church in the next village.'

Ana knew that her husband didn't have a high opinion of this group, but Stefan couldn't deny that the church was growing in size and reputation, even if he was sure that most of the people joining the new fellowship were already Christians who were dissatisfied with their church life in another place.

'These younger people from our church think that we should buy a drum kit, use guitars and only sing praise songs composed in the past twenty years. But I don't think that the style of music is the real problem,' said Stefan.

'Why is that, my love?' asked Ana.

'Well, I admit I like the music. But when I've sung those songs at our national conference, the words don't seem to be very deep and the music often comes from America so the tunes don't match the rhythm of our beautiful Romanian language,' Stefan explained. 'And if I don't feel at ease, I'm sure that most of our older members would stop trying to sing them at all.'

They reached Ana's uncle's home so the conversation could go no further. Stefan turned off the engine and they went inside to greet him.

As they sat down with their cups of coffee, they couldn't stop Ana's uncle from talking. He had recently come back from a business trip to America and Japan. He was a great storyteller and the time went quickly.

'I remember in Japan there wasn't a piece of litter anywhere on the ground. I accidentally dropped a sweet wrapper and a young man picked it up, bowed to me and gave it back to me as if I had lost my wallet! But there's no place like your own country,' he added. 'That's where you feel at home. That's where you understand the unspoken words in a conversation, where you know the customs and what's expected of you.'

As they drove home, Stefan was more relaxed. He was relieved to have an answer to his questions.

'You see, Ana,' he explained, 'church revitalisation can't be done in a cultural vacuum. An American televangelist can't communicate deeply with a Romanian. Our church has had to change and become more relational. It's had to change to be more aware of today's issues. But we must keep the good stuff – the things where we feel culturally at home.'

On the way home in the car, they enjoyed listening to some Romanian folk songs and sang along with them heartily.

14

Working towards lasting change: leadership

On the revitalisation flow chart (see chapter 5), I call this final stage of the revitalisation process 'working towards lasting change' with the main objective being 'putting good leadership and decision-making systems into place'. They inevitably go together. I have already quoted Ed Stetzer who wrote that, 'Leadership was rated as the number one factor by the churches that experienced revitalisation.'[1] So what is leadership? And how can we improve our leadership?

The aim of leadership has to be the glory of God (1 Corinthians 10:31; Ephesians 1:6, 12, 14). It is not fundamentally a question of organizational techniques. Instead, it means loving and serving others and living for God.

Leaders should have a clear-sighted and realistic view of the present condition of the church and a clear picture of a desirable future situation. They should be capable of defining that reality in a way that others accept and of offering a map of how to reach this projected outcome. Someone once said to me, 'If you want to know if you're a leader, look over your shoulder.' In other words, is anyone following your lead? In revitalisation, as in other fields, the objective of leadership is to achieve something by inspiring other people to participate actively. In short, this will happen when a leadership team with different skills forges an exciting vision in the minds of the congregation and then encourages and reassures people that it will come into being: 'Yes, we can get there together!'

For the revitalisation process to be successful, leaders need to develop a set of skills. First, you must learn how humans function. The Bible contains more than just doctrine. It also gives valuable insights into

---

1 Ed Stetzer, *Comeback Churches: How 300 Churches Turned Around and Yours Can Too* (Nashville, TN: B & H, 2007) p. 34.

human nature through wisdom literature (such as Proverbs) and a wealth of stories in both the Old Testament and the New Testament. We learn about people primarily by being involved with them, sharing life together and observing how they react in different circumstances but an academic or psychological approach can also be useful. Some people have learned a lot about themselves and others by using diagnostic tools such as the Myers Briggs Type Indicator to gain insight into their personality traits and working styles (personally, I have found this very useful). Others learn by watching films or reading fiction. As a graduate of literature, this is often my first port of call.

Second, it is important to understand your own culture. This can sometimes be difficult because you are immersed in it. As the saying goes, 'we don't know who first discovered water, but we're pretty sure it wasn't a fish.'

Third, you must try to understand the decision-making processes in your church. Where, when and how are decisions made? The processes may need to be changed as the revitalisation process moves forward but, in the first instance, you have to use what is there. You must be aware that the formal decision-making process in the church may not be the way in which things are truly decided. This needs real discernment. This informal authority is relational, rather than something officially recognized, and it can be used positively or negatively. Some people see themselves as 'gatekeepers' and find ways to prevent suggestions (or even decisions) about change that they dislike. Sometimes they have no formal authority (for example, they are not members of the church council) but they try to maintain a quiet influence among members when it comes to voting for change. They may be involved in the practical organization of certain aspects of church life and hang on to their influence in these areas. Leaders need to identify the gatekeepers and make sure that their influence does not override the formal authority and decision-making processes in the church. Informal authority can also be used in healthy ways, increasing trust among the members and within the revitalisation team. Through building positive relationships, you can win people round and accelerate change. Still, you should bear in mind that informal authority can be less visible and less accountable, which brings dangers, and it is important to resist the temptation to bend the rules or manipulate people to drive through change.[2]

---

2 I recommend Marcus Honeysett, *Powerful Leaders?: When Church Leadership Goes Wrong* (London: IVP, 2022) for further reading on formal versus informal and legitimate versus

Fourth, you should prepare your written documents with care. Ask other people to look at them carefully before communicating them to the church as a whole. Are they clear? Does the main argument hold together coherently? Is there any vocabulary that could hurt or offend someone?

Finally, however many people have their say in a church meeting, ask God to give you the gift of synthesizing ideas, summarizing and suggesting creative compromises so that you reach some concrete conclusions at the end of each meeting.

Resistance to change

This leads us to the hardest part of church revitalisation. Sooner or later, there will be some opposition to change. This can even lead to conflict within the church because, for some people (or even many people), change can bring a sense of loss similar to a bereavement. The analysis of the process of mourning proposed by the Swiss psychiatrist Elisabeth Kübler-Ross can help us to understand this. She proposed a five-stage model that explains the emotions that people experience as they go through the change process. I have observed the same order in the church revitalisation process:

1. Denial: 'No! We don't need to change!'
2. Anger: 'After all these years, I don't want to change!'
3. Bargaining: 'Can't we keep some things the same as they were before?'
4. Depression: 'I can see that change is inevitable, but it makes me feel sad and insecure because everything will be different from what I've known until now.'
5. Acceptance: 'OK, I'll go along with this and I'll do my best to make it work.'

What can the revitalisation team do when they are faced with this reluctance to change? I have gleaned (and used) several ideas over the years. First, you must recognize that the sense of loss that I have just mentioned is very real. According to research, in every branch of human activity (the church is no exception), fear of change stems primarily from what is known as 'loss aversion'. This is explained in great detail in the

---

illegitimate use of authority.

international best-seller by Daniel Kahneman, *Thinking, Fast and Slow* in which he demonstrates that losses loom larger than gains. It is thought that the pain of losing is about twice as psychologically powerful as the pleasure of gaining. People are more willing to fight to avoid a loss than to make a gain. Here is a typical example from the book:

> You are offered a gamble on the toss of a coin. If the coin shows tails, you lose $100. If the coin shows heads, you win $150. Would you accept it?[3]

Experimental data shows that nearly everyone would refuse. The fear of losing is more intense than the hope of gaining. In a church, people are used to doing things in a certain way and often fear new ideas, even if the ideas are suggesting something positive. A change in worship style, the introduction of home groups or the use of technology might well be considered to be necessary improvements but may nevertheless be opposed or resisted. The anxiety at the thought of losing something on the way to change is very powerful. I believe that the only answer is the gospel. The centrality of the gospel seems to be the best way to combat loss aversion:

> But whatever were gains to me I now consider loss for the sake of Christ. What is more, I consider everything a loss because of the surpassing worth of knowing Christ Jesus my Lord.
> (Philippians 3:7–8)

When church members see what is important, when they understand that new ways of doing things can help them to know Jesus better, the feeling of loss aversion can be considerably reduced.

Second, in communicating the vision, acknowledge openly that you understand these fears while conveying the necessity of change to prevent the eventual disappearance of the church. Remember the fundamental principle: people change when the pain of not changing is greater than the pain of changing.

Third, try to identify what lies behind the opposition. This is not always easy to discover. The French philosopher Blaise Pascal wrote that, 'The

---

3 See Daniel Kahneman, *Thinking, Fast and Slow* (London: Penguin, 2012) p. 284.

heart has its reasons that reason cannot know.'[4] What is the real issue? It could be fear of the unknown. It could be a misguided desire to remain faithful to those who have gone before (which may include parents who were influential in the church). It could be the apprehension of no longer having a role in the church. It may be the anxiety of losing a rhythm of life that had become comfortable.

Fourth, focus on ideas and concepts to avoid things becoming personal. You are not fighting against people ('flesh and blood') but against, 'the powers of this dark world and against the spiritual forces of evil in the heavenly realms' (Ephesians 6:12). You want to take everyone with you (or at least as many as possible) and this will not happen if they feel ridiculed or if they do not feel respected as people.

Fifth, speak in private with people who feel that they have a responsibility to protect the group from bad influences. As we mentioned above, these gatekeepers can have a power greater than their formally recognized authority and they have some potential to block change. In the revitalisation process, they may feel that they have not been consulted enough. They may feel that what is being suggested is a passing fad and believe that things will return to normal if they stand their ground. They need reassurance. You can say, quite genuinely, 'I share your concern,' because there is often a grain of truth in their perception and others may well be thinking what the gatekeeper is saying aloud. It may well be possible to incorporate some of their ideas in the revitalisation strategy without compromising what is essential and this can win over the doubters. It is good to have a positive attitude: 'The ideas of these people can, in fact, enrich our project.'

Sixth, always use moderate, peaceful language in presenting the revitalisation strategy and in conversation with individuals. For example, 'I agree with you there', 'That is a wise suggestion', 'Is this the right time?' 'Have you considered?' The aim is to preserve our unity, which is a great achievement in itself in a world that sometimes seems to be full of hate. As Christians, we should be happy to be together and to discuss how Jesus can be glorified in us as a church.

Finally, leaders must be diplomats in the best sense of this word. This can sometimes be misunderstood by Christians because we are called

---

4 Author's translation. See Blaise Pascal, *Pensées*, Brunschvig Edition, fragment 277.

to be fundamentally honest and to shun manipulation in proclaiming the gospel:

> We have renounced disgraceful, underhanded ways. We refuse to practise cunning or to tamper with God's word, but by the open statement of the truth we would commend ourselves to everyone's conscience in the sight of God.
> (2 Corinthians 4:2 ESV)

Nevertheless, Jesus commended the dishonest manager because he acted shrewdly – 'for the people of this world are more shrewd in dealing with their own kind than are the people of the light' (Luke 16:8) – and he taught his disciples to be 'as shrewd as snakes and as innocent as doves' (Matthew 10:16). What does it mean to be shrewd and how far can we go down this path? The dictionary definition is to be able to judge a situation accurately and turn it to your own advantage. Other words to express the same thing are 'wily' or 'crafty' but these may not be as acceptable according to your understanding of what they imply. It is legitimate to achieve an aim by being strategic and using the tricks of the trade. This is not necessarily unspiritual, especially in a fallen world, as long as the motivation under-girding the action is love for people and desire for God's glory. Again, I would stress that we should make sure that we are not doing this in a way that is manipulative or an abuse of power. We want to be persuasive in advocating for change but, at the same time, we should be quick to listen and give room to other people's ideas.

Here are a few illustrations that the revitalisation team may find useful:

- Take people by surprise. In other words, take an unexpected path and go where people are not expecting you to go. Consequently, they will not know how to object to your proposals. Jesus gave us a good example in answering questions about whether a Jew should pay taxes to the emperor (see Luke 20:20–26) or where his authority came from (see Luke 20:1–8). Here is a contemporary example: if someone says to me, 'What you are proposing is worldly. It's the world's methods,' I answer, 'On the contrary. I believe that the world has borrowed our biblical methods because they are true to human nature and have stood the test of time.'

- Watch out for good opportunities. Whenever someone says anything in a discussion or at a leaders' meeting that goes in the direction you want to go, jump on the opportunity to say that you agree. This shows that you are not alone in having this idea and that others can also make important contributions.
- Praise what is already happening and suggest that something else would be an interesting addition instead of a straightforward replacement. Vocabulary is important here. If someone says that this new activity will divide the congregation, you can suggest that it is, in fact, multiplying the church.
- Choose your battles. Not everything is worth fighting for.
- Never forget the ultimate weapon: 'Let's try it for six months. If it doesn't work, we can always stop the experiment.'

Lasting change needs commitment and tenacity at the same time as loving care for the church members. Being a pastoral leader in a church going through a period of revitalisation calls for particular skills and the desire to go on learning for your whole life. It may mean dialogue with a health professional, a banker or an IT worker in order to draw good applications from the Bible texts that you are about to preach from. It may mean having lunch with church members in or close to their workplace to get to know them better in their daily life. It may mean seeking out organizations who may be able to help a church member who has a difficult personal problem. But it will never mean losing the priority of 'prayer and the ministry of the word' (Acts 6:4).

In today's world, lasting change always means putting good leadership and decision-making systems in place. According to your church history and the culture that you are in, there has to be a good balance between power and authority in the church. Power is situated within the legal and structural framework of the church. It implies the duty of abiding by the rules that society has decreed for all citizens (for instance, safety in the church building and transparency in financial matters) and is generally ensured by an elected church council or board that can be monitored by the members. Authority concerns the pastoral team who are recognized by the congregation in order to teach, guide and pray for the life of the believers. In some countries, according to their national laws or cultural expectations, such pastoral work may be subject to the same rules of confidentiality as those that apply to lawyers or doctors, so information gleaned in pastoral counselling should not be shared with the elected church council or the pastor's spouse. It is important to be sensitive to your cultural context and to make sure that there are healthy standards, shared expectations and clear teaching around power, authority, confidentiality and related issues.

Collegial leadership is both biblical and effective but two requirements are necessary for a team to achieve a common goal and ensure lasting change:

- clear decision-making processes in the church (more churches are divided over this than I dare to think about)
- good processes of delegation including choosing the right people, communicating clearly what is expected of them and mentoring them appropriately

The next chapter will look at some practical issues that arise from the concept of a healthy church.

A small town near Manchester, UK

'How can you believe in something you can't see?' Tom's colleague, Josh, knew that Tom was a Christian and asked his question as they were driving together to a meeting in central Manchester.

Tom smiled inwardly. They had started teaching on current issues and apologetics during the morning services in the church because the survey of church members had shown that many of them didn't know how to talk about subjects like this in an appropriate and non-aggressive way. The different invited speakers had all pointed out how important it was to be plausible as Christians in what we say and the way that we say it.

Trevor had been one of the speakers. With his literary training, he had given a talk based on the *Pensées* of Blaise Pascal, the seventeenth-century French mathematician and philosopher. Pascal became a Christian at the age of thirty-one and wrote down his thoughts, hoping to make them into a book that would convince his free-thinking friends. He died at the age of thirty-nine before he could complete the project. Tom remembered one extract very well. Trevor had even printed it out and suggested that everyone stuck it on their fridge door as a constant reminder:

> Men despise religion. They hate it and are afraid it may be true. The cure for this is first to show that religion is not contrary to reason, but worthy of reverence and respect. Next make it attractive, make good men wish it were true, and then show that it is.[1]

In other words, first surprise and disarm non-believers by showing them how relevant Christian faith is to us in our daily lives and how it fulfils all of people's aspirations, even in this postmodern age.

Just two weeks previously, a visiting evangelist had addressed them on the very subject that Josh had brought up, so Tom felt that he knew what to say. That led to an excellent discussion on their way to the meeting. He asked Josh about things he believed in that he hadn't seen directly. He explained that the Bible gives eyewitness testimony from people who had seen God revealed in the historical figure of Jesus.

In the course of the conversation, Tom was surprised to learn that Josh had noticed their church building for the first time only a few weeks before. He

---

1 Author's translation. See Blaise Pascal, *Pensées*, Brunschvicg Edition, fragment 187.

often drove down that road going to his sports club and had noticed that they had cleaned up the building and installed a new electronic noticeboard. At first Josh had thought that it was a bit gimmicky but then he said to himself, 'Why shouldn't a church keep up with the times?'

Before they parked the car, Tom invited Josh to come along to church one Sunday morning when he didn't have a match at his sports club. Because of the changes in the way they ran the Sunday morning services, he had no fears that Josh would find it boring or irrelevant. 'And why don't you bring your wife along too? My wife, Jane, would be pleased to meet her and we could all go out for a meal afterwards.'

Josh promised to think about it. He had never expected such a provocative question to have such an outcome.

A city in the west of France

As luck would have it (or it would be better to say that it was in God's providence), Valérie and Myriam worked in offices quite close to each other. They often met up for their lunch break at a nearby snack bar that offered healthy food at a very reasonable price. One day, they came across one of Valérie's colleagues, Laura, who happened to be having lunch there. She asked if she could join them and they started chatting about the bus strike that was threatened for the following week.

After a few minutes, Laura asked how they knew each other and Valérie explained that they went to the same church.

'You go to church?' exclaimed Laura. 'I don't believe it! I've always thought of you as an intelligent, vivacious woman. Sorry! That sounded awful. It's just that most of the people I know who go to church seem to be so dull and narrow-minded.'

'That's OK,' Valérie reassured her. 'I'm used to hearing that sort of thing. There may be a grain of truth in it, but I see a big difference between being a churchgoer and being a Christian. I wasn't even brought up by believing parents. In fact, my Dad calls himself an atheist.'

Laura was fascinated. 'So how did you become a Christian, then?'

'Oh, it's a long story, but it was when I was at university. There was a Christian group in our department and they invited me to go along to their meetings and discover the Bible.'

'But weren't you afraid it might be some sort of sect?' Laura couldn't help but ask.

Valérie's answer explained everything. 'No, not at all. I already knew one of the guys who went to the group and I knew that he wouldn't get involved in anything suspicious.'

Laura wasn't finished. 'I've always heard that Christians are very prejudiced and that you're all homophobic. One of my best friends is a lesbian and she's always telling me horror stories about Christians.'

Valérie gathered her thoughts. She didn't want to be misunderstood. 'Well, there may be a grain of truth in that too, but one of the most important things that Jesus asks us to do is to love others as much as we love ourselves. That's a big ask, but how can we hate homosexuals if Jesus asks us to love them?'

Laura was determined to get to the bottom of this question. 'But you do believe that homosexual relationships are wrong, don't you? How do you deal with that?'

At their church, they had had several teaching sessions on such issues, so Valérie wasn't caught off guard. 'We believe that God's gift of sex is for a man and a woman in the context of marriage. That's what we try to follow as Christians. And that's not always easy. You may not believe this, but I didn't have sex with my husband before we were married.'

'Wow! That is unbelievable,' exclaimed Laura. 'But I'm intrigued. I'd like to hear more. Couldn't we start a weekly Bible discovery meeting, just like the one you had at university? We could meet here and sit in a corner. I'm sure no one would mind.'

A village in central Romania

At the high school that Alexandru and Mihai attended, there was a small but noisy group of students who called themselves 'progressives' and advocated for diversity and care for the environment. They were very active on social media and they watched a lot of videos online. Many of these were in English, which they didn't always fully understand. Most of the other students were much more traditional and held more conservative views. Alexandru and Mihai didn't feel that they could identify with either group. As Christian teenagers, they had come to see that their faith was radical, not conservative. But they also saw that there were clear moral guidelines for humans as created beings and that these reflected God's very character.

One Monday morning, the school was in an uproar. The radical students were calling on all the students to come out on a symbolic strike one day a week to call attention to the danger of global warming, hoping that this would bring politicians to see it as an urgent issue.

As it happened, Alexandru and Mihai had participated in a conference at their church two days earlier. Their father had invited a Christian who was working in the field of nature conservation to come and help the church to think about the question of ecology in light of the Bible's teaching. This expert had reminded the audience that God is our creator and that sin has harmed the relationship between humans and the environment so that, according to Romans 8, the whole of creation is groaning right up to the present time. However, we as Christians are looking forward to a new heaven and a new earth where righteousness will reign, as Peter writes in his second letter.

'Hey, you two!' shouted one of the radical leaders when Alexandru and Mihai walked through the school gate. 'Come over here. What do you think about this strike we're trying to organize?'

The twins went over to talk with the group. Mihai was the first to speak. 'Well, as Christians, we think that environmental questions are very important.' Some of the group scoffed and one of them said that he had never heard a narrow-minded, reactionary churchgoer say such a thing. Mihai didn't back down. 'It makes sense that we should be interested in ecology because the God we believe in created the whole universe in the first place. It's obvious that we should look after this planet he put us on.'

'But I don't believe in God,' stated another member of the radical group.

Alexandru responded by saying, 'Then on what grounds do you say that something is right or wrong? You remember the book we were studying last term, *The Brothers Karamazov*? It explored the theme that if God does not exist, then everything is permitted.'

Mihai added, 'You're being illogical as far as I'm concerned. If we're just another animal that happens to have evolved greater intelligence, then we don't have any particular responsibility to care for the planet. But if we're made by God to be stewards of creation, we do have that responsibility. You're right to feel that we should take care of the world but you don't have a consistent reason why.'

'Yeah, well, human civilization will collapse and millions will die if we don't save the planet! That seems a good enough reason to me,' said someone at the back of the group.

Alexandru replied, 'I don't think that we can save the planet, as you say. We all have to face death in the end. One day, God will put an end to the world as we know it and judge us all but between now and then we'll do our best to look after this world. Just like an old person keeps looking after themselves, washing and dressing properly, even though they know that they're going to die soon. But Jesus died and came back to life to give us a hope beyond death, for us and for the planet.'

The radical group found themselves caught between two emotions: irritation and amazement. 'So are you going to join the strike or not?'

The twins said that they wouldn't. They suggested creating an ecology group in the school, which could act locally but also remember the effects of global warming on vulnerable populations.

'Our church is collecting money to help plant trees in Burkina Faso to stop the encroachment of the Sahara. Couldn't we all raise money for that?' suggested Mihai. 'And maybe you could come along to our Sunday meetings and find out more about God's love for the world.'

15
Working towards lasting change: practical issues

As various groups of people have discovered the models of gathered and scattered church, they have asked me many interesting questions. This chapter is a response to a certain number of misunderstandings and an attempt to bring more clarity to some aspects of the model.

The scattered church

I am not using this expression in the sense in which it is found in some New Testament texts when the Jerusalem church was scattered after the martyrdom of Stephen. The believers were forced to leave the city and scattered throughout Judea and Samaria (see Acts 8:1–4). Later, we learn that they went as far as Phoenicia, Cyprus and Antioch, sharing the gospel even with the Greeks, in other words, with non-Jews (see Acts 11:19–20). In his first letter, Peter writes to 'God's elect, exiles scattered throughout the provinces of Pontus, Galatia, Cappadocia, Asia and Bithynia' (1 Peter 1:1).

In this book, however, scattered church is a theological term used to express the life lived by Christians where they live, work, study and play, as opposed to their time together in the gathered church where they meet to worship and learn how to live as Christians in today's world.

This distinction became all the more stark during the Covid-19 pandemic. Some people referred to online video meetings as the scattered church but, in my opinion, it was still the gathered church even if the Christians were physically apart because they were together for a set time as a break in their ordinary life.

Visibility

How can the church be visible in a postmodern, secular world? For whatever reason, we do not have much coverage in the secular media. Apart from trying to improve our contacts with the media, what visibility can we aim for?

First, visibility refers to our church building. That depends on its location and its historical place in the community. The external appearance is important. The noticeboard should look modern and be kept up to date with information about the activities in the church.

Second, visibility refers to the presence of the church in the community. After all, a church is primarily a group of people and not a building. To what extent are members of the general public aware of the existence of the church? Do the local authorities know the pastor? In France, the minimum expectation is that the pastor is on the list of people invited to ceremonies (for example, Armistice Day) or to the inauguration of new public amenities. This visibility is increased when the church organizes its own public events such as art exhibitions or lectures on subjects of topical interest. In my church in Paris, for example, we took the 500th anniversary of the Reformation as an opportunity to organize an exhibition and a series of talks. It is important to invite local authorities such as the mayor and the member of Parliament to these events. Even if they do not come, they become aware that the church exists and that it does interesting things.

Third, visibility refers to the presence of Christians living daily as the scattered church in close proximity to non-Christians. This is a corrective to the gathered church aspect of our ecclesiology and a necessary one because, traditionally, much weight has been placed on attracting people to our events and to our place of worship. This can still be relevant today, but a real effort has to be made to communicate to the congregation that they have an important role to play as missionaries, which means (quite literally) people sent out into their day-to-day environment. After all, that is the only place where Christianity will be visible for the vast majority of people around us.

It is a well-known fact that when non-Christians come to an event based in a church building today, it is generally because they have been invited by a Christian whom they know from their relational network. That said, we should not underestimate the value of the physical church building and a church association set up according to the legislation in your country. These can reassure non-believers that they are not setting foot in a cult.

Social action

The place of social action in a church has been notoriously difficult to define, ranging from the absolute prioritization of evangelism on the one hand to the prioritization of social justice on the other, via the equal partnership between evangelism and social action as expressed in the Lausanne Declaration[1] or in the ideas of integral mission that are often developed today. This book is not the place to enter into these theological and ethical discussions, despite their importance. Personally, I think that the material and spiritual sides of our lives have equal importance as far as the Bible's teaching is concerned. However, what is eternal has more importance than what is temporal. When it comes to church revitalisation, the leadership team will have to think about the relative place of the gathered and scattered sides of the church in the two areas of evangelism and social action.

As we saw in the section on the visibility of the church, social action organized by the local church may be seen as a positive activity. We are called to love our neighbours and people's perception of Christianity may be more positive when they see our good works: 'they may see your good deeds and glorify God' (1 Peter 2:12).

However, there are dangers and limits. People may think that we are exploiting the needy to bring them into the church. This is a fairly common attitude in some countries of Europe as social media spreads fake news and unproven accusations. This is the case all the more in postmodern culture in which people distrust those who try to impose an overarching explanation of life because of the fear that they will use every possible means to impose their norms on others. In addition, though political action is a necessity, a church should be careful not to become associated with a political party.

---

1 The following extract gives a summary of the position taken in the article: 'Although reconciliation with other people is not reconciliation with God, nor is social action evangelism, nor is political liberation salvation, nevertheless we affirm that evangelism and socio-political involvement are both part of our Christian duty.' From The Lausanne Covenant (1974), Article 5, 'Christian Social Responsibility'.

In light of these dangers, there are three possible solutions:

1 The local church can encourage its members to become involved
   in social or political action as individuals with a clear Christian
   commitment, without identifying this as the party line of the church.
2 The local church can become involved in a parachurch
   humanitarian project. This could be at a local interchurch level
   (for example, serving homeless people) or it could be as part of
   a national or international organization (for example, Tearfund,
   which works in the field of international development to bring an
   end to extreme poverty and injustice, or A Rocha, which works for
   nature conservation and other ecological issues). Such organizations
   need partners on the ground to raise awareness and funds and to
   work at the grass-roots level.
3 The local church can set up an organization to run church-inspired
   actions. For example, our church in Paris ran a Fairtrade shop that
   also sold Bibles and Christian books. It was situated next to our
   place of worship and we did not hide the fact that the shop was
   run on a Christian basis by Christian volunteers.

Personally, I think that it is important to be able to conceptualize the difference between the primary call of the church and its social implication in order to express it publicly. At a speech given in the presence of the local authorities when we opened our Fairtrade shop, I explained that Christians all through history have believed that sin has entered the world, cut us off from a relationship with God and led directly or indirectly to a great number of social problems. We call this the fall. The church exists to enable people to get to know God again and social action exists to reduce the harmful consequences of the fall. Non-Christians seem to understand this kind of explanation.

Does the scattered church only concern individuals?

The short answer is no, scattered is not synonymous with individualistic. For a start, we live as a scattered church in small groups as couples, families, students sharing a flat or as a group of young people spending time together. There may be more than one person from the local church working in the same company and they can meet during the week for fellowship or to share the gospel with their colleagues. I have always been moved by the simple words of Jesus in John's Gospel, which I have already quoted in this book: 'A new command I give you: love one another. As I have loved you, so you must love one another. By this everyone will know that you are my disciples, if you love one another' (John 13:34–35). Although most people will not have the opportunity to see this at work in the whole of the body of Christ as the gathered church (which is a pity, as they would see how the love of Christ enables us to love each other despite huge differences in our temperaments and backgrounds), at least they might see this in the more limited context of a small group of Christians.

The scattered church is the ideal place to live out the organic nature of the church. One possible way to do this is by encouraging people who live in the same district of your town to think in terms of local initiatives for shared mission. What do I mean by this? It could be as simple as being a non-threatening but visible group of Christians in their neighbourhood who meet occasionally to pray for their neighbours and who sometimes organize events (for example, a table tennis tournament or a quiz night). They may sometimes invite their friends round for a meal to spend quality time together while praying for opportunities to share something of the gospel.

However, these organic and unstructured groups should not be confused with initiatives that are often put in place by churches such as home groups for Bible study and prayer. These are institutionally organized and thus part of the gathered church. These groups often develop very strong relationships between the members and this can make it very difficult for a newcomer, especially a seeking non-believer, to join and feel part of the group. That said, some home groups can be very effective initiatives for shared mission if they are aware of this difficulty and work hard at being welcoming.

Evangelism

The paradigm change implied by the emphasis on the scattered church might be intimidating to many Christians. Instead of seeing evangelism as an activity organized by the institutional church, it becomes a way of life in which a Christian lives out and, when possible, speaks out about their faith in Christ.

I was recently speaking to the leader of a student group in the south of France. He was telling me that the students he works with are sometimes frightened of being visible and audible witnesses to their fellow young people. They are afraid of being mocked or of being seen as intolerant, concerned that they might be violating university regulations in some way and anxious about being asked questions to which they do not have the answers. They preferred the leader to organize apologetics evenings to which they might (perhaps) invite their friends.

Many of these students come from Christian families and, paradoxically, this may explain why they are so apprehensive about revealing their Christian identity. I remember reading an article by a Christian journalist several years ago. In summary, he wondered how we can explain our indifference towards sharing the gospel when we were brought up in a Christian environment. He pointed out that, in a sense, we are both fortunate and unfortunate to have been brought up in the Christian faith: fortunate in having all the answers to the great 'whys' of our existence but with the misfortune of getting these answers before we had asked the questions.

For years when I was working with Christian students, I tried to encourage them to be natural, to spend time with non-Christians, to give their point of view in discussion (without necessarily becoming involved in long-winded explanations) and to ask questions in order to understand the points of view of other people. Realistically, this requires three levels of input from church leaders:

1 To help Christians become so amazed by the gospel and so in love with God that they cannot keep their mouths shut. Hopefully, our church services will do this.
2 To help Christians discover their true identity in Christ so that they are not ashamed to be who they are. A colleague of mine in student ministry recommended that Christian students look in the mirror each morning and repeat three times, 'I'm a Christian and that's OK!'
3 To help Christians say things in a way that their non-Christian friends will find plausible so that they can begin to understand the true implications and meaning of Christianity in terms they can identify with.

The final chapter will discuss the outcomes of the revitalisation process and the need to create a culture of ongoing change.

16

Working towards lasting change: strategic issues

As we come to the end of this book, my prayer is that many churches in the UK and across Europe will find new and authentic spiritual life as they go through a process of revitalisation.

To summarize this book, five factors will contribute to a local church regaining its health. Just as when you pack your suitcase before going on a journey, this is a checklist to see if anything is missing in your reconnection process:

- Vision. The vision of a healthy church, approved by the members, is the foundation of the whole process.
- Motivation. Understanding and accepting the vision is essential for motivating church members to work on the action plan and to keep moving forward through the whole revitalisation process.
- Strategy. Some sort of action plan or strategy for change must be drawn up by the revitalisation team with the active participation of church members.
- Discipleship. The heart of the action plan is discipleship in the social, societal and spiritual areas. This is where the fire of change is fuelled.
- Networking. This refers to all types of coaching from outside of the church. This may be put in place formally by the denomination with a facilitator and include regular meetings with other leaders of churches involved in revitalisation. Alternatively, it may be a whole range of informal types of encouragement, such as relationships with like-minded people, the support of a healthy church nearby or interaction through social media, visits or conferences.

If any of these components are missing, the end result may be very different:

- Without vision, the end result will be confusion.
- Without sustained motivation, there will be resistance to the process.
- Without a clear strategy for change, false starts are likely.
- Without discipleship, anxiety about reaching the objectives will ensue.
- Without networking, people can become discouraged.

In other words, here on earth with our human limitations, we need to bear all of these factors in mind in order to reach the goal of a healthy church. And, for there to be genuine spiritual change, we must also recognize the necessity of earnest prayer and the Holy Spirit's work among the church members, while being aware of these human dynamics.

Outcomes of revitalisation

As we think of how we can work towards ensuring ongoing change, it is helpful to take a realistic look at the various possible outcomes of the revitalisation process.

The worst-case scenario is that the church decides not to enter into the process. They do not see the need for change and there is already too much inertia. A pastor stuck in this situation may well decide that it is time to move on to another place of ministry.

Alternatively, the denomination or the revitalisation facilitator may help the church to die well. This may be because the church building is in a rural area where very few people live and amalgamating with another local church is the best way forward. Or it may also be that there is a flourishing evangelical church situated just around the corner and it makes more sense to combine funds and energy. The closure can be done in a positive way. Everything that the church has accomplished can be celebrated, another church can be found to welcome the few remaining members and the property can be sold, for example, to purchase a building for a new church plant.

The church may also close temporarily in order to reopen with new leaders who can use the premises with a new mission strategy. This is sometimes called 'replanting the church'.

Finally, the church can decide to change its premises or move to a new location in the town in order to start up again in a more visible or accessible place.

The next three outcomes are the most desirable (and the most probable) by the grace of God:

1 The leaders and members are motivated by the new vision of a healthy church and the Christians are supported and accompanied by their denomination and/or a facilitator as they go through this process of change.
2 As above, but with the help and support of a new pastor.
3 A healthy church supports and helps the struggling church in practical ways as it embarks on the revitalisation process. It can offer resources and even send a few people from their membership to become members of this church. I must stress that the motivation for this change must come from the existing members of the church that needs revitalisation, otherwise this outside help will be counterproductive.

That said, we do not yet live in a perfect world and we must remember that every church is made up of sinners who are forgiven but not yet totally sanctified. There may be mixed results. A church may grow in health but some people may hold back because they are unwilling to change. Leaders need to focus on progress and not perfection and work prayerfully for the long-term strengthening of the church through ongoing change.

A culture of ongoing change

How is it possible to have this longer-term vision? The important thing is to persevere in the revitalisation process in order to create a new culture of ongoing change. At various stages, it is easy to think, 'We have arrived,' and slacken our efforts. We need to be on guard. Some people have the gift of seeing when the church is going round in circles or slipping back into old ways and we should encourage them to speak up when necessary.

At least one important change a year will help to set the tone, though this should also be done carefully. It should not be change for change's sake but adapting to a new need that we have seen in the previous year.

An intentional way to do this might be to draw up a formal strategic plan. It would be premature to do this at the beginning of the revitalisation process, though of course we have been talking about building a strategy for change right from the beginning of this book. Once a church is going in the right direction, the church members will be better able to see the logic of longer-term planning to ensure sustainable growth in both quantitative and qualitative terms. The aim is to ensure that the church is both healthy and effective.

In order to avoid falling back into old routines, a strategic plan will proceed in three stages. First, the *mission* of the church (in other words, the long-term reason it exists) should be clearly stated. This will include both scriptural and contextual elements. Our church in Paris wrote down our mission statement in this way:

> Living as a church in such a way that each member will grow spiritually in the knowledge of our Trinitarian God 'to the praise of his glorious grace' (Ephesians 1:6). Spreading the gospel to Parisians in our contemporary context.

Other churches may want to write their mission statement in a much more detailed way.

Second, the *vision* is where you want to be within a certain time scale (for example, in five years' time). What are your hopes for the church? It might be helpful to look at this in terms of the church building, the staff, training programmes, Bible teaching, the church's prayer life, meetings, commitments to the wider community of people around the church or in terms of the church's contextualized relevance. In short, how do you see the church giving an equal weight to the gathered church and the scattered church in your environment?

Third, the *strategic plan* is what you can do towards achieving this vision of the church. What practical steps can you take? God alone can do certain things, such as bringing someone to repentance and faith. But you can decide certain things, such as training church members to communicate the gospel with clarity and tact in their professional spheres. Two things are essential as we can see at the end of the revitalisation flow chart (see chapter 5). The leadership must discern what can be done intentionally and what can just be committed to God in prayer. And they must continually evaluate whether members are being helped to grow spiritually and to reach out with the gospel.

As we reach the end of this book, after discussing many practical details, I would like to remind you of what is essential: revitalisation concerns the vision of a healthy church leading to a process with three simultaneous aspects, spiritual, social and societal. We should never lose sight of that as we work and pray for the revitalisation of our churches.

In this book, I have tried to be faithful to the Bible both in terms of what it teaches and the emphasis that it places on the church as a gathering in which Christians are taught and trained, built up and encouraged in order to live their daily lives to the glory of God and for the salvation of others. I find it interesting that today's society makes this emphasis indispensable. Europeans are more and more indifferent towards Christianity, which makes the 'come and see' approach to evangelism more difficult than the 'go and show' approach. But this does not detract from the essential role of the local church as a company of believers. Whether we approach the question of edification and evangelism from a biblical point of view or from a pragmatic one, we arrive at the same conclusion in today's world, all over our European continent.

To encourage us all to undertake this process of revitalisation, may this verse from the Old Testament inspire our prayers for God to raise up a generation of leaders of the same calibre: 'from Issachar, men who understood the times and knew what Israel should do' (1 Chronicles 12:32).

The vision of a healthy church is absolutely essential. 'This is love: not that we loved God, but that he loved us and sent his Son as an atoning sacrifice for our sins. Dear friends, since God so loved us, we also ought to love one another' (1 John 4:10–11). My hope and prayer is that churches all over Europe will be healthy, growing and taking their place in the spread of the gospel both in their own country and to the ends of the earth.

The man whom Paul calls 'our dear friend Luke, the doctor' (Colossians 4:14) ends Acts in the same upbeat manner: 'He proclaimed the kingdom of God and taught about the Lord Jesus Christ – with all boldness and without hindrance' (Acts 28:31).

Ultimately, my prayer for reconnected, revitalised churches is none other than for the glory of Jesus: 'We pray this so that the name of our Lord Jesus may be glorified in you, and you in him, according to the grace of our God and the Lord Jesus Christ' (2 Thessalonians 1:12).

Further resources

Books

From an American perspective

- Harry L. Reeder, *From Embers to a Flame: How God Can Revitalize Your Church* (Phillipsburg, NJ: P&R Publishing, 2004).
- Ed Stetzer and Mike Dodson, *Comeback Churches: How 300 Churches Turned Around and Yours Can Too* (Nashville, TN: B & H, 2007).
- Thom S. Rainer, *Autopsy of a Deceased Church: 12 Ways to Keep Yours Alive* (Nashville, TN: B & H, 2014).

From a European perspective

- John James, *Renewal: Church Revitalisation Along the Way of the Cross* (Leyland: 10publishing, 2016).
- Neil Hudson, *Scattered and Gathered: Equipping Disciples for the Frontline* (London: IVP, 2019).
- Marcus Honeysett, *Powerful Leaders?: When Church Leadership Goes Wrong* (London: IVP, 2022).

On change management

- John Kotter and Holger Rathgeber, *Our Iceberg Is Melting: Changing and Succeeding Under Any Conditions* (New York: Saint Martin's Press, 2006).

Websites

- You can find copies of the charts and diagrams used in this book at www.revitalisation.fr/en/strategy. This is a bilingual website (in French and English). Click on the correct flag on the home page to select your language.
- Information on the European Leadership Forum and the Church Revitalisation Network can be found at www.euroleadership.org.
- See www.foclinitiatives.org/yrm-church-revitalization for more information on the Year-Round Mentoring programme.